BUYING
COUNTRY
PROPERTY

BUYING
COUNTRY
PROPERTY

Pitfalls and Pleasures

IRVING PRICE

Illustrations by Grambs Miller

HARPER & ROW, PUBLISHERS

New York, Evanston, San Francisco, London

FIRST EDITION

STANDARD BOOK NUMBER: 06-013408-9

LIBRARY OF CONGRESS CATALOG CARD NUMBER: 71-161637

To all those, including you, the reader, who have given me a beautiful and exciting reason for getting up every morning

CONTENTS

PREFACE

You're interested in acquiring country property, so we'll want to give you a relaxed and realistic way to search for that place in the sun—be it for sanity, serenity, security, investment or self. The reasons are your business. Ours is seeing that you have the education and expertise with which to make this step. We both care. We care a lot, if you'll pardon the expression.

We'll leave the arguments, pro and con, why cities are dying, suburbia a myth, to the experts. We are not sociologists or economists. We only know there is a tremendous "return to the land" syndrome apparent all over the country.

Whether you're in the market for a manicured estate, or just a cottage small by a waterfall, the name of the game is "know what you're doing." Otherwise, you could end up "it" in a baffling game of blind man's bluff.

We know what we're doing: trying to remove the cloak of secrecy surrounding the buying of country real estate. So let's take it off!

IRVING PRICE

BUYING
COUNTRY
PROPERTY

1

LET'S GET ACQUAINTED

It is not our intention to stimulate the "buying of country property," but assuming you are either in process of, or anticipating the move to the countryside, to expose all of the ramifications of acquiring it.

The pitfalls are many—as plentiful and as common as dandelions in a field—but not as obvious. What lies ahead in our book is not Top Secret to those of us who were born, raised, and lived all of our lives in the country. However, it will serve as an overflowing well of information for you. One that you could not normally tap in the routine course of purchasing property from the seller, his agent, or the Madison Avenue brochure.

Country folk do not try to deceive you or mislead you. The pitfalls there they accept, live with and take for granted as part of their way of life. You, too, may accept them; but before you do, you should know that they are there!

Pitfalls, like poison ivy, should be recognized and avoided. Don't touch, if you are susceptible and ultrasensitive!

We both know the many reasons why this migration from the city is taking place. One of our goals is to shorten the distance for you in time, energy and costs on your trip from metropolitan U.S.A. to a country home.

The time we will spend together will encourage some; possibly, it will discourage others, but we hope by the end of our association that you will have become a more sophisticated buyer: that you will be able to fulfill your dreams, hopes and aspirations without the disappointments, frustrations and unnecessary costs that often accompany the novice or the ill-informed.

I want our relationship to be extremely comfortable for you, because I know generally what most of you are hoping to find, in both the tangible and intangible, in your trip to the countryside. I feel confident we can relate to thousands of city dwellers and that our marriage is going to be most compatible.

You're going to be told exactly as it is! So, if the roof leaks, you'll know it now, not after you move in. We will be emphasizing more of the pitfalls than the advantages. You must become involved in your country project, with its many phases that are unique to purchasing real estate in rural areas, that can be best known only to those consistently involved with same.

The terms used and the subjects covered are generally applicable to most rural areas throughout the United States.

We both know that this project in your life is a giant

step, involving a major change in your living habits and routines, to say nothing of being a substantial investment and obligation. I want this to be a very pleasant and rewarding experience for you. During the course of our journey together, if there are questions that remain unanswered, or subjects you wish clarified, do not hesitate to write. It is the least I can do in appreciation of the time, expense and interest you have shown in reading this book.

We are assuming you have already made up your mind to buy. We are not telling you that you should. The country is not a Utopia, but it is a place where you will find a meaningful freedom, where people have not forgotten how to smile, and where sound is birds and brooks—not noise!

The sages from the cities, who have been reaching out

for the country over the past few years, brought with them their words of wisdom by the wagonload. Are yours the same?

- I don't want to see the house from the road, nor the road from the house!
- I want to get up on a Sunday morning, take my chidren by the hand, and walk for an hour on my own property without coming to a fence.
- I want neighbors, but I don't want to see them.
- I want a place where I have privacy, but not isolation.
- I want to sunbathe in the nude.
- My life needs a balance—a little of each—city and country.
- I want to combine a place in the country with investment.
- I need some grass again.
- I don't want to send my daughter to the kind of school where I teach.
- We want to have a closer communication with nature.
- We want the best of two worlds for our children. The city for close cultural advantages, but we want them educated in country ways.

We are going to try to narrow the distance between the spoken word and the written word to a common bond of communication. For this reason, I strongly suggest that you review the glossary of real estate terms that you will find in Chapter 26. Your general knowledge and understanding of them in advance will help eliminate the curves and bumps while we travel the country roads together.

Don't run off scared. It's easier than you think.

2

YOUR REAL ESTATE
CONSULTANT

Your guide to the selection and purchase of your country home is as important as a safari leader on a trek through the jungle. Therefore, select your broker carefully. The well-established, highly reputable, substantial real estate firms will relieve you of untold burdens, details and responsibilities that are part of the purchase of country property. As many personal confidences must be exchanged throughout every phase of a transaction, long, personal friendships will develop between you and members of the brokerage office.

A good broker will prove invaluable in obtaining mortgage financing, negotiating the many extras, baby-sitting with your children while you're inspecting properties, arranging transportation and, above all, finding exactly what you want in space, acreage and price range. Most states strictly enforce laws protecting the purchasers of real estate in their dealings with real estate brokers. Further,

5

you will generally find a high degree of professionalism throughout the industry.

It is rare that a first appointment will result in your finding your dream house. Actually, the first day spent with your broker gives him an opportunity to observe your likes and dislikes, and learn what will "turn you on." From that day forth he will be waiting, and looking, for the listing that will satisfy your needs. A series of phone calls, letters and photographs will follow the first meeting and you'll look forward to the next visit with great anticipation.

Viewing country properties can be a very exciting and stimulating experience. But there are certain steps that must be taken to avoid frustrating and time-consuming jaunts. First, select your brokerage firm from among names you've gotten from local banks, chamber of commerce offices or well-known law firms. These brokerage firms that specialize in real estate usually have well-established, full-time offices. Call or write for an appointment, describing your basic requirements. Be as prompt as possible in keeping your appointment as the brokerage office will have given a great deal of time and effort establishing appointments with owners of property they plan to show you.

Discuss the financing of your anticipated purchase with your broker, such as the amount of cash available for a down payment, and the type of mortgage you would desire. Many firms waste the time of their clients in showing properties listed for amounts far in excess of the potential buyer's financial capabilities or desires. Confidence must be shared. If for any reason you do not feel this confidence with your broker from the start, then change firms.

Don't be discouraged or disillusioned if you haven't

found the right place after three or four showings. The limit of time available is the main reason people become uncomfortable as they look, so try to allocate as much time as you can to these visits.

Until you have narrowed your selection to a few possibilities, it is not wise to have an entourage of friends and relatives accompany you. It's also a good idea to have as open a mind as possible in looking for country property. Experience clearly dictates in both marriage and in property selection that you usually end up with just about what you had in mind in the first place.

The more successful brokerage firms are the ones that really "level" with you from beginning to end. You will find in the country communities that it's much more important to brokerage firms that a new and lasting friendship is established with their client than that a deal is immediately consummated. Business survival in small communities is dependent upon reputation and referral. One bad mistake or unfortunate relationship with a client is one too many.

A most common form of making contact with a broker is through an advertisement in a newspaper or a brochure on specific types of property. Firms that consistently advertise through these media are well-established and reliable. Major metropolitan newspapers will accept advertisements only after investigation authenticates the credibility of their advertisers.

The term *realtor* is used extensively in identifying real estate brokers. It is a coined word which may be used only by an active member of a real estate board affiliated with the National Association of Real Estate Boards. It does not necessarily hold true that any broker not a realtor is less

qualified or reliable. There may be a multitude of proper reasons to explain why he is not a member of a local board affiliated with the parent group. However, the term *realtor* does designate professional standing in a real estate organization of high professional standards and ethics.

There is no national policy to which brokers adhere on obtaining mortgage loans for their clients. Many firms negotiate the mortgage requested as a matter of courtesy, while others charge a fee for obtaining the mortgage for the client. The size of this fee depends upon the amount of the mortgage and the effort expended to arrange it. It is recommended that you discuss mortgages with your broker before submitting a formal application to a lending institution.

One of your broker's chief responsibilities is to bring

about a meeting of the minds between you and the seller, leading to a preliminary agreement as to general terms. He is well trained and experienced in all phases of the negotiations. You should *not* communicate directly with the seller of the property during any phase of the transaction without the knowledge and permission of your broker.

The fees or commissions paid a real estate broker are usually the responsibility of the seller. Therefore, the broker is not entitled to represent both the seller and purchaser, receiving a fee from both, without all parties of the transaction agreeing in advance. Although it is not a common practice, the broker can represent the interested purchaser only and be paid by him, in the event the buyer assigns him the sole responsibility of selecting a particular piece of property.

An agreement to buy can collapse when the purchaser personally negotiates with the seller on items such as furniture, tools and equipment. I have witnessed extremely desirable real estate transactions explode because of an argument over a kitchen set with a market value of ten dollars. Conclude the real estate portion of the transaction before bargaining for end tables and the rug in the hallway. If the grandfather's clock and living-room drapes catch your fancy, advise your broker accordingly and let him be the middle man.

Before actually taking title, you will find dozens of reasons to call your brokerage firm. They will serve you well in taking care of many routine matters such as notifying the utility company, the post office, the insurance firm, and those needing to be present at the closing.

There are always those intrepid characters who feel they can save a brokerage commission by seeking out the country property themselves, and dealing directly with the owner. Forget it. The owner will charge you the same price and keep the commission cream on top for himself. In the law profession there is a word of advice to attorneys: "An attorney who represents himself is a fool!" These wise words apply well to the idea of negotiating for property yourself, without a broker.

The broker in most instances technically represents the seller and is compensated by him. But he cannot function unless you, the purchaser, are satisfied. To this end, he will do his utmost to negotiate a fair and equitable sale between buyer and seller. Never hesitate to make a respectable offer below the listed price. It is up to you to start the transaction, letting the broker have something concrete to start negotiations with. If you are enchanted with a property and anxious to become the next owner, remember money talks. So advance a check to your broker of a nominal amount as evidence of good faith. This offer, if accepted, would be contingent upon such things as obtaining mortgage financing, good title, survey and approval of any or all contractual obligations by your attorney.

If your physical inspection of all potential possibilities of properties proves fruitless, your current broker may refer you to another broker in the community to continue your search. If he does not voluntarily do so, simply ask him to extend you this courtesy. His briefings to you of a referral broker will save you both time and wasted effort.

The purchaser of country property usually finds the broker who sold him his property continues to be one of his best country friends.

3

SELECTING
AN ATTORNEY

We strongly recommend a "country" attorney to represent you in all phases of purchasing country or rural
property. The term "country" attorney, of course, is a
misnomer, as lawyers who practice in country or rural areas
are extremely sophisticated, usually very well trained in
and competent to handle the many phases of general law
practice. Real estate transactions normally represent a substantial part of their practice, and they are well acquainted
with all the ramifications involved in buying country
property.

Most local attorneys have been born and raised in rural
areas. They are well known to their colleagues, banks,
brokers and the general community. They are particularly
well equipped to handle unique problems that may arise
during the transaction, either personally, or by phone, right
on the spot, thus saving a good deal of time and expense.
In many instances, the attorney representing you will be-

come a personal friend and guide you in your selection of contractors, well diggers, painters, plumbers, gardeners, etc.

The purchase of your country property is a major one, involving literally dozens of legal aspects. **Under no circumstance obligate yourself in writing without first discussing all angles of your proposed purchase with the attorney you have selected!**

Your real estate representative is licensed by the state in which he has the right to function. Certain states have passed strict legislation to protect your interests. However, some states do allow brokers to prepare certain legal documents. I caution you not to sign any form without first consulting your attorney, regardless of how simple it may appear on the surface.

There are many standard forms of "memo purchase agreement" or "binder agreement" that merely serve as a sign of good faith on your part when accompanied by a nominal deposit, often termed "earnest money." The purpose of these instruments is to give the seller an indication of your definite interest, subject to an attorney's review of same, preparing a formal contract, obtaining mortgage financing, title search and other conditions that have to be met and agreed upon by both parties. If you are absolutely certain that execution of this type of instrument does not legally obligate you, or subject you to the loss of your "earnest money," then proceed accordingly, but be certain that these two factors are clearly stated.

The average purchase will involve the attorney's making a title search, reviewing the contract to purchase and conveyances relating thereto, assisting with the mortgage application, and being present at the closing of the transaction. His responsibilities will vary, depending upon the problems involved, and the legal fees to be expected are of course in accordance with the amount of time and effort expended. Naturally, you will discuss in advance with him the approximate fee to be charged. This will eliminate any misunderstandings at the time of closing.

I am well aware that many of you have relied upon your own metropolitan attorney, who has been your long-time counsel and friend, and you feel uncomfortable and reluctant in selecting a stranger to represent you. If this be the case, discuss the entire matter with your legal counsel and request he select or recommend a local attorney in the area where your property is located.

Local attorneys are usually most cooperative and understanding. They will keep your city attorney informed of each phase of the transaction. Many metropolitan lawyers do not wish to become involved in direct representation in purchases of this type, because of the inconvenience of distance and their unfamiliarity with local problems.

You may also select your local attorney from a roster readily made available by banks in the area, local bar associations or real estate brokers. You may have a friend or relative in the area, happy to recommend someone who has represented them to their satisfaction.

You will find that it is rather important, for many reasons, that you become "involved" in as many aspects of local activities as possible, and become an integral part of the community, whether residing full- or part-time in the area. It is for this reason that I recommend local counsel, as well as local people to furnish you with all possible goods and services you may require.

4

WHAT ABOUT
A SURVEY?

Most country properties having been owned by the same family for several generations, consisting of substantial acreage, have *not* been surveyed by a licensed land surveyor or engineer. In fact, a great percentage of all country property sold in the last twenty years has not been properly surveyed and, further, accurate maps of these properties don't exist.

A typical deed to a hundred-acre farm or land parcel will state something like this: "Beginning at a point of a tall elm tree in the northeast corner of the property, then proceeding along a stone wall bounded by lands of Smith to a point marked by a pile of rocks, then westerly along a stream bounded by the lands of Jones to a large red barn owned by Green, etcetera and etcetera, being one hundred acres, more or less."

This description was fully acceptable seventy-five years ago, but today the elm tree is no longer standing, the stone wall has been removed, the pile of rocks was plowed under, the stream has dried up, the red barn burned down thirty years ago, and Smith, Jones and Green have long since gone to their reward.

The owner now in possession unequivocably reports to you that he has one hundred acres, and no one has ever questioned what he believes are his boundary lines. One of the easiest ways for you to antagonize and infuriate this type of seller is to insinuate that the parcel might be less than one hundred acres; or that you and your attorneys have reason to believe the adjacent owner claims part of either the road frontage or one of the parcels involved to be his land.

Farmer Brown, the seller, is not about to pay for the cost of a survey, and is usually not too receptive to the idea of giving you the month or two of grace that it would take to employ a licensed surveyor to substantiate the acreage involved by the undertaking of a survey and mapping of the land. This problem, as stated above, has now become an everyday occurrence and probably the most significant factor in all country transactions today.

The more sophisticated seller is well aware that the emphasis is more on the acreage and less on the buildings. Many lending institutions, title insurance companies, and attorneys are making it mandatory that a survey map substantiate the parcel to be conveyed. Federal, state and local agricultural agencies are aerially mapping vast areas of country property. These maps have served as a guideline in the absence of a formal survey or adequate description.

Some deeds are so vague and incomplete in describing parcels that it becomes impossible for the licensed land surveyor or engineer to undertake a formal survey and

certify that it is accurate. This problem can only be solved by establishing with all bordering property owners what is known as a "boundary line agreement" wherein all parties legally agree to the establishing of property lines.

The sellers are becoming more aware that if they warrant a certain number of acres that they are selling, they could be subject to substantial litigation, in the event that the purchaser proves by survey that certain acreage purchased was considerably less than stated in contracts and deeds.

Real estate firms today are extremely cautious in stating

the number of acres that they are selling, unless there are certified maps available. Brokers are doing their utmost to convince sellers to have a survey undertaken before the property is publicly listed, in order to avoid complications.

One acre of land, seventy years from now, when our population is expected to reach one billion, so say the statisticians, might be worth literally thousands of dollars. For this reason, and for many others, **you should have in your possession a survey, certified by a licensed engineer or surveyor, of the parcel you intend to buy, before closing the transaction.** You are making a large investment. In the absence of a very descriptive deed or map, you are inviting problems for yourself, for your children, grandchildren or heirs, when the time comes to sell the property.

Title insurance is discussed in another chapter. However, you should realize that title insurance policies usually *do not* insure the acreage, nor guarantee your acreage without a certified map and "boundary line agreements" by all owners bordering your property.

It may appear to you that I am becoming extremely technical in this matter of survey. But I am concerned not only with the present, but for the future, when a blade of grass might represent a small fortune.

Undertaking a survey represents the same type of protection as having fire or liability insurance on your buildings. The cost is nominal and will vary, depending upon the section of the country and the problems involved. A ball-park estimate of a survey without many major problems could range from $1,200 to $1,700 for a one-hundred-acre parcel. The surveyor that you engage will be more than willing to estimate in advance the approximate cost. Thus, in the event that your attorney advises you that he is not satisfied with the current description of the property, and that a survey should be made, by all means be guided by his judgment.

Costs of surveys today are in many instances borne equally by seller and purchaser. The contracts recite that in the event the survey reveals less than the acreage represented, the purchaser has the right either to withdraw from the contract, or to see that the purchase price be adjusted. The seller may ask to have inserted in the contract a statement that, if the acreage results in more than what was represented, the price be increased accordingly by agreement.

There is an extreme shortage of available licensed surveyors and engineers in most country areas and a great demand for their services. The shortage presents a major problem in closing the transaction within a reasonable period of time. In many areas severe winters increase the time needed by surveyors, although, as we said before, various parts of the country have aerial surveying services available. The aerial equipment is very costly so that work done by this means is very expensive.

Some old descriptions contain reasonable, accurate information from which a "deed plot plan" may be made. "Deed plotting" is preparing a diagram or sketch of the property involved from the information contained in the deed to the parcel. The deed may recite the distances as to frontage, depth and other peripheries, with reference to various landmarks as points of beginning and ending, the names of bordering neighbors, roads or highways. This map or drawing may or may not be prepared to scale and the sophistication of the finished product is dependent upon the extent of information contained in the deed, plus the ability and experience of the person preparing it.

Many present property owners possess this type of map or sketch and often refer to it as their "survey" of the property. *It is not a survey!* If you accept this rather meaningless document as a formal survey, then the blind is leading the blind.

We must recognize that for many years customs surrounding the transfer of property in country areas added up to this: what should have been done and what the procedure *was*—"A horse of a different color!" The temperament and attitude of both buyer and seller determined the results. There is no substitute for a certified survey. Be guided by the recommendations of your attorney and your own personality as to whether less precise plans will do for you. A formal survey means insuring your investment. You will be spending many thousands of dollars for the purchase and improvement of your property. Doesn't simple good judgment dictate that you know exactly what you are buying and where it is?

Many areas of our country today are undertaking the preparation of tax maps and assessments of acreage by towns, villages or counties, and property evaluations and boundaries are being guided accordingly. This step forward is a giant one and in time to come will expedite the sale of tracts of land and property.

5

MONEY, MONEY, MONEY

The link between your dream and reality in buying country property is money. (Darn it!) Before you start looking, three key questions must be answered:

1. How much of your own money do you wish to spend?
2. How much money do you wish to borrow?
3. How much money are you willing and able to repay monthly, quarterly or annually?

Your definitive answers to these questions will determine the price range of the property you are seeking. Further, it will make available or eliminate the particular type of property you would like to buy.

If you are in a position to pay all cash (this might be regarded as un-American), the process is a simple one and the continuation of this chapter would be pointless. However, the majority of you will become involved in financing your purchase—so let's explore the world of finance that awaits you.

The most common and "conventional" way of financing real estate is to borrow money from a banking institution, savings-and-loan association, insurance company or private individual over a period of years. The borrower gives the lender a mortgage as security for the loan. The mortgage is a formal document that creates a lien upon the real estate for payment of the debt. The borrower pays for the use of the money obtained a percentage of that sum known as *interest* which varies in amount depending upon the normal money-market conditions. The repayment of the debt is usually made in monthly installments for an agreed specified period of years. In the event that the borrower fails to meet his obligation, the lender may legally take the real estate and sell the property involved to satisfy the unpaid balance of the obligation.

For example:

Total cost of property to be purchased	$25,000
Own funds available	5,000
To be borrowed, known as a mortgage	$20,000

Conventional mortgage financing available from major banking institutions and other loaning agencies usually requires the borrower to have from 20 percent to 35 percent of the total purchase price of the property available from their own resources before they will consider loaning the balance of from 80 percent to 65 percent of the amount required to consummate the purchase. This conventional type of financing usually requires the borrower to repay in monthly equal installments of both principal and interest the sum borrowed over a period of fifteen to twenty-five years.

The monthly payment to repay $20,000 computed at 7 percent interest over a period of twenty years would be approximately $155.06 per month. The same amount computed on the basis of twenty-five years would represent a monthly payment of about $141.36. Interest is computed upon the amount owing of the principal balance at the end of each month. Although the monthly payment remains the same, the net result is that a bit more of the total monthly payment is being applied each month to principal and less to interest as the principal balance is continuously reduced. Naturally, the longer you wish to take to repay the $20,000 the less the monthly payments will be, but you will be paying substantially more in interest costs.

If you wish to make your own computation for amounts less or more than $20,000, based upon a twenty-year repayment schedule at 7 percent interest, you may do so as follows: for every thousand dollars of borrowed money the monthly cost approximately for principal and interest will be $7.76.

A majority of loaning institutions require the borrower to pay monthly one-twelfth of the total property taxes and one-twelfth of the property insurance in addition to the principal and interest. These amounts are added to the regular principal and interest payments and the lending institution pays, on behalf of the borrower, his taxes and insurance as they become due throughout the years. This relieves the property owner of his responsibility to meet these payments personally. The funds set aside for taxes and insurance each month are placed into a special bank account known as an *escrow* account.

Conventional mortgage financing by institutions is usually *not* available for the purchase of "raw" or "undeveloped" land without buildings. Bank policies and many state laws limit the placing of mortgage loans to "on established property." A borrower will find it extremely difficult to obtain conventional mortgage financing for property that is not generally well improved and modernized. The abandoned farm or home type structure without good plumbing, central heating, modern electricity, etc., will have little or no chance of passing inspection approval. The lending institution will probably advise that it might consider an application if the applicant wishes to improve the property first with his own funds and thereby meet the minimum requirements for consideration.

The right to repay in all or part the mortgage obligation before it becomes due, at any time during the term of the mortgage, must be a written consideration between borrower and lender. **Be sure you have this right to do so and determine if that right is so granted with or without a penalty sum. No prepayment penalty is to your advantage!**

Many banking institutions charge a sum of money for granting a mortgage, payable only once at the time the mortgage is granted, and computed upon the amount granted. This "extra cost" is known as *points*. Two points for a $20,000 mortgage would be $400. Try to avoid the institutions that require this extra sum.

The tighter the money market, the greater the possibility that you will have to become involved in paying these points.

It is general banking procedure to issue annually a statement to the borrower of all pertinent information pertaining to the mortgage activity for the statement period involved. The amount applied to principal, interest, taxes, insurance and various balances remaining will be clearly defined. These statements are extremely valuable in the preparation of income-tax reports. Your attorney will explain in detail all the various terms of your mortgage obligation. You should familiarize yourself with your rights and obligations pertaining thereto.

Many individuals who are selling their property wish to take back a mortgage in part payment of the total purchase price of the real estate. If the seller does not require more cash down than you are able to advance, you should give consideration to this method of financing, providing the terms are within your budget. If the seller does take part payment of the purchase price in the form of a mortgage, this is known as a "purchase money mortgage." There are many tax advantages to the seller by going this route if he is selling his property at a substantial gain. Sellers who are extremely desirous of disposing of their real estate property that does not meet normal conventional bank financing may have no other alternative than to offer financing themselves. This is especially true in the sales of "raw" or "unimproved" land.

Bank or institutional type of financing is the most recommended method, if available. Private financing presents potential problems in the area of continuity of both borrower and seller, estate problems, misunderstandings of payments due; it is usually of shorter duration in terms of years to repay.

It is to your distinct advantage to have the right under prearranged conditions to have a portion of the mortgaged property released from the mortgage lien in the event you wish to dispose of a portion thereof by sale or transfer. Let us assume that you wish to erect a home or other building on a portion of the property under mortgage. It would be impossible for you to obtain clear title or new financing for this project unless that portion of the property was released from the original mortgage.

Most conventional mortgage agreements will require that you fully insure the mortgaged property and the buildings located thereon, against all known perils. In the event of destruction of any of the buildings, the insurance proceeds must be used to replace within a reasonable period of time the buildings lost or damaged, or the insurance proceeds will be paid to the institution or individual holding the mortgage as reduction of amount owed.

The normal procedure to obtain a conventional mortgage loan involves the filing of an application with the lending institution. The real estate broker or attorney will prepare the application from information you supply. The application usually involves submitting a statement of your financial condition (all that you own and all that you owe, in detail), employment and personal data, credit, banking and personal references, and statement relating to amount to be borrowed and repayment schedule of details in reference to your proposed purchase, including purchase price.

The lending institution will make an appraisal of the property, review your credit status, and issue a notice of rejection or commitment usually within thirty days from the time of making application. Although mechanically very sophisticated, rural banking is extremely personal. My suggestion would be that you take the time to meet the bank officers personally. They have a deep regard for community obligations and it is to your advantage that a personal relationship develop from the start. It will provide the bank with an opportunity to react to a human being, not just an application. It may seem like a time inconvenience, but it certainly is worth the effort. Do not expect the bank to act as your appraiser without submitting a formal mortgage application. It just is not usually done.

Most financial institutions do not reveal to the borrower their opinion of market value in the event the mortgage application is denied. Local bank policies, attitudes and appraisals do differ. It is for this reason that you may have to make more than one application for financing, if your first attempt is unsuccessful. Certain banking institutions specialize in conventional mortgages, while others are more concerned with commercial type financing and do not cater to the mortgage business. Be guided generally by your real estate broker or attorney in all phases of financing your purchase.

Metropolitan area banks do not usually wish to become involved in out-of-the-area financing unless they have branch facilities available in the community in which you anticipate purchase. Most rural areas are served well by local financial institutions and are desirous of satisfying the needs of the people coming into the community.

You may be assured that the contents of your mortgage application and credit information will be thoroughly investigated. *Don't gild the lily or give misinformation!* Take the time and effort to explain the reasons for any unfavorable credit history. Many times there are logical and reasonable explanations for what might appear on the surface to be damaging evidence.

Answer promptly all correspondence from the mortgage application. Be sure to write a thank-you note or make a personal phone call to the banking officers upon receipt of notice of approval of the application. Little things mean a lot in the country.

Federal law requires that the borrower execute what is known as a *"disclosure statement."* The loaning institution itemizes all interest and other charges and the borrower acknowledges this information by executing this statement.

The loaning institution will place particular emphasis on the cash or liquid position, the income, present debt status, and past banking experience of the applicant. Many borrowers take the position that, if the property is substantial, the loaning institution is not taking any risk if they have the property as security for the loan. The lenders are concerned with protection, yes, but are equally adamant in their decision not to become involved with delinquent or troublesome mortgages. Foreclosing a mortgage and constant requests for back payments are costly and annoying procedures for loaning institutions. The ability of the borrower to pay from current income or reserve funds in the event of illness, unemployment or economic

recession is a primary provision of the loaning institution.

Although it might be substantial, the income of a young wife is generally not considered in the buyer's ability to repay or gross income, as it may be generally assumed that she is "vulnerable."

The mortgage officers considering an application will be specifically interested in determining the availability of the total cash for down payment and closing costs needed by the applicant at the time of closing of the transaction. The financial statement must reflect that these monies are either in a bank account or will be available from the sale of bonds, securities, insurance policies or similar easily convertible assets.

The borrowing of sums needed to provide the down payment and closing costs from other banking institutions or sources is usually frowned upon and not well received in reviewing a mortgage application. This condition is not applicable to those who wish to place securities as collateral for down-payment funds.

Conventional mortgage financing is available to those of you who wish to build a new home or substantially recondition an older one. The borrower presents the plans and specifications to the bank for approval and requests a commitment in accordance with loaning policy. The usual procedure is that an agreement is entered into whereby the lender advances the money to an owner with provisional payments at certain stages of construction. This agreement is known as a "building loan agreement." Simultaneously, the borrower executes a conventional mortgage. This method provides the money needed to pay the contractor during construction.

Those seeking conventional type mortgages but who are unable to meet the normal down-payment requirements of 20 percent to 35 percent have the opportunity of making application for certain types of Federal Housing Administration (FHA) approved plans, GI, Farmers Home Administration loans, and other federal or state home-financing programs that are available. Those programs require as little as 15 percent to no down payment. They give consideration to annual income, size of family, military service record, but they do limit the maximum conventional mortgage available.

The purchase of land for agricultural use and related activity may be financed through various federal and state agencies that provide liberal repayment programs. Dairy, fruit, Christmas tree, vineyard, citrus grove, beef cattle, poultry, sheep and other associated operations are the types of farms that these agencies cater to. The extent or scope of involvement does not have to be substantial in order to qualify. The borrower, however, must indicate a genuine interest and have the ability to repay obligations from outside sources until the particular farm operation becomes self-sufficient. Inquire from your broker or attorney as to the location of the nearest office of the agencies making these loans.

Financing your purchase in a retirement or planned community development that is well established is usually a rather simple process. The financing institutions involved will grant a commitment to the borrower upon receipt and approval of the personal credit investigation. Well in advance of making financing available to the buying public, they will have satisfied themselves as to property values, reliability of developers, credibility of contractors involved, appraisals as they relate to the project. You will usually find their terms attractive and consistent.

The availability of most conventional mortgage type loans for the purpose of purchasing "raw" or "unimproved" land depends upon community banking facilities and their interest in this particular type of loan. These loans, if granted, are usually of short duration (one to three years). They should be considered by those who are anticipating a quick resale or building at a future date. The loan will be considered primarily on the basis of the financial statement of the applicant. It may be granted on a secured or nonsecured basis, depending upon the bank policy.

Do not lose the opportunity of closing a transaction to property that you want simply because you lack the immediate cash down payment, assuming the cash needed will be forthcoming within a reasonable period of time from an estate, bonus, pending sale of other property, sale of securities, insurance proceeds or litigation settlement. If you can determine with reasonable certainty the amount and date of expected receipt of anticipated funds, you will usually not have any major difficulty in borrowing from a commercial bank the amount needed, with the understanding that these funds will be repaid upon receipt. This method provides you with the ready cash to proceed with your purchase. Most commercial banks will consider extending this type of loan for a period of up to one year without the formality of collateral.

Be prepared to provide documentation of the conditions surrounding your anticipated sum of money as evidence of your good faith.

Most conventional type mortgages will remain constant as to the interest rate charged for the entire period of the mortgage. In other words, if prevailing interest rates increase, you will not be obligated to any more than your original commitment. On the other hand, if prevailing interest rates decrease, your rate will still remain constant as originally committed. You will, of course, have the option to refinance your mortgage at a lower interest rate, if available, but concern must be given to whether the cost of refinancing will be to your long-range advantage.

It may be possible for you to assume the present mortgage and all terms thereunder from the seller of the property you are buying, providing the balance to be assumed and the cash that you have available to pay the seller will equal the total purchase price. For example, the seller owes the bank a balance of $15,000 on his present mortgage. He wishes $25,000 for the property. If you are prepared to pay $10,000 in cash and assume his mortgage, it will close the transaction with a minimum amount of expense and time. The advantage of assuming a mortgage will be a substantial saving in closing costs, application fees, mortgage tax, legal fees; and you might be fortunate enough to be assuming a mortgage at an interest rate less than the prevailing rate for new mortgages. Many banking institutions do not permit another to assume a mortgage without the permission of the bank. They do not usually grant this permission before reviewing in detail the credit of the new owner. If the prevailing interest rate is higher than the rate being charged on the existing mortgage, it is not very likely they will grant permission to assume unless the new owners agree to the prevailing interest rate.

Those selling property whereby the mortgage is assumed by the buyer should do so only if the lending institution will release them in full from all obligations, present and future, under the mortgage terms. If a buyer assumes a mortgage and the lending institution does not release the seller, the contingent liability remains with the seller until that mortgage is paid in full. Familiarize yourself thoroughly, whether you are buyer or seller, with all details involved in this regard by consulting with your attorney before acting.

One of the main problems involved in financing purchase of real estate whereby the seller holds the mortgage ("purchase money mortgage") is that the seller does not usually want to extend to the purchaser a long period of payment, such as twenty to thirty years. This places upon the buyer an extreme hardship in making substantial monthly, quarterly or annual payments. The purchaser might be in a better position financially five years hence, but unable to cope comfortably with this obligation during the early years of the mortgage. Consider this alternative as a more reasonable approach to private financing if conventional bank financing is not available to you for one reason or another. Request that the mortgage be granted on the basis of a twenty-five-year payment schedule with the right of the seller (holder of the mortgage) to request the balance in full remaining at the end of five, ten or fifteen years. This will give the seller certain peace of mind, assuming he has need for the entire sum to meet unexpected contingencies along the way. Elderly folks are always naturally concerned that they might have need for large amounts of money for medical and other purposes.

This method gives the borrower the opportunity to breathe easily for five to ten years with comfortable monthly payments. He will be in a much better financial position at the end of five or ten years to obtain conventional bank financing in the event the mortgage is "called" at the termination of the agreed-upon period.

Private financing at times provides for the payment of interest *only* (no principal payments) for the first three to five years of the mortgage; the entire sum or amortization of principal and interest to commence thereafter for a specific number of years. Particular attention should be directed to the provision granting the right to prepay the principal sum at any time during the term of the mortgage. This is extremely important in the event you wish to sell all or part of the mortgaged property and the purchaser demands title free and clear of any and all encumbrances, liens and mortgages. If this provision is not included, it might not be possible for you or your family to dispose of the real estate involved.

If you become involved in private financing, request that your attorney obtain several copies of the schedule of payments for the life of the mortgage. These schedules, computed by financial organizations and available for a small fee, detail the allocation of principal, interest and balance remaining at the end of each payment. Copies should be part of a permanent record for your attorney, family and the individual or individuals to whom you are making your mortgage payment. This procedure will eliminate any misunderstandings along the way.

Do not make the last payment on the mortgage until you receive a formal document executed legally by the individual or individuals holding the mortgage that your obligation is paid in full.

This document is known as a "satisfaction of mortgage" and must be recorded to clear the records accordingly. Con-

sult with your attorney before making your last payment
and he will advise you accordingly in this regard.

Most private mortgages or financing do not provide for an
"escrow" account. The responsibility for the payment of all
real estate taxes and insurance rests directly with the owner
of the property, if the seller does not want to become
involved with the obligation of these details. Develop a
very methodical and punctilious habit in paying all obligations of a mortgage promptly when due or, better yet, a

bit ahead of time. A good credit history of punctual mortgage payments is a great asset when seeking additional credit or consideration in the event of financial involvement.

There are many areas of the country that are *not* served well by convenient, conventional, liberal banking facilities. Investigate thoroughly the banking attitude prevailing in the area in which you are seeking property before spending a great deal of time and effort in your search for an investment. The difference required in down payment from just one county to another—a distance of only ten or fifteen miles—might be as much as 20 percent to 30 percent, or possibly financing would not be available for some property. This condition exists simply because of the availability of banking facilities and the size of these institutions within the banking district involved.

Real estate brokers are extremely conscious and well informed as to the maximum financing available within any area in which they function. Discuss all financial goals in detail with them as Step Number One.

Financing substantial improvements to your established property after you have closed title may be done conveniently without refinancing your mortgage or disturbing a good interest rate. Banking institutions provide home-improvement loans or other types of financing for these purposes on a convenient repayment program, usually up to five years. The money needed for siding, a new roof, fireplace, additional bathroom, or other improvements should be obtained without disturbing the mortgage. Personal loans are available for these improvements, too.

May I recommend consideration be given to obtaining what is known as "mortgage life insurance" that is usually available from the banking institution holding the mortgage or from a private insurance company. A minimum monthly sum (varying with age of applicant and amount of mortgage) will provide that the balance of the mortgage due will be paid in full in the event of death of the head of the household. The monthly payment remains the same over the term of the mortgage. It is reasonable peace of mind precaution. All details are available from the financing institution or your own private insurance company.

In the event of extended disability of the borrower, insurance is now available at a very nominal cost providing for the entire monthly payment due the bank for the length of time of the disability. Discuss the advantages of both the death and disability mortgage insurance coverages with your attorney and banker.

Funds needed for cash down payment and closing costs may be obtained from sources other than one's savings or checking account. Many families have accumulated a substantial amount of cash value in life insurance policies over many years. These funds are readily obtainable from the insurance company on a loan basis at very attractive interest rates. I would *not* recommend that these policies be terminated or cashed in by the purchaser. Borrow the funds available directly from the insurance company. This option keeps the policy in full force and effect during the time of the loan. The borrower usually does not have to repay the loan in any specific installments and will be liable for interest payments only.

If ready cash is a problem for closing purposes, you may also give consideration to offering other personal assets that a seller might accept as down payment, such as works of art, jewelry, stocks or bonds not readily marketable, antiques, autos or boats, or even one's annoying relatives.

Should I obtain a mortgage larger than necessary, if I have the funds available to close the transaction? Should I repay my mortgage in advance, if I can afford to? Why should I obtain a mortgage in any amount if I have all the necessary funds to pay for my purchase in full?

The answers to these frequently asked questions are dependent upon a multitude of circumstances applicable to each family's status and personality. Expert banking, legal and accounting advice should be sought before reaching any decision in these areas. Every involvement in today's complex world affects one's income-tax status. Interest costs in regard to purchase of real estate are presently deductible under federal and most state tax laws. Depending upon the tax bracket, it might be to an individual's advantage to obtain the largest mortgage available with resultant substantial interest deductions.

Your own available funds might produce a more attractive return invested in your business or other investments, making it more sensible to borrow the maximum for the purchase of real estate, keeping funds active in other endeavors bringing a return of invested capital far in excess of additional interest cost for borrowed funds. The personality of the principals involved might dictate that a large cash balance be readily available for any emergency or contingency; therefore, don't let's use these funds for the purchase of real property.

There are thousands who adhere to the school of thinking that inflation is going to continue in our society. The principle involved in their theory is that one should borrow the maximum and repay the obligation with "cheap" dollars as the inflationary spiral continues.

Every family's anticipated future needs that appear to be certain and determinable—for example, college costs or major purchases such as automobiles, that would be taken from savings and not current income—must be considered before such funds are allocated for the initial real estate purchase. Estate planning should also be reviewed before any giant steps are taken.

We must recognize there are those who do not wish any debts whatsoever, even though there might exist many tax and other advantages for their being. The "pay-as-you-go" philosophy must be respected, accepted and admired. To those who still firmly believe in this almost nonexistent theory—do your own thing and God bless you!

Give due consideration to the several comments in reference to the questions above as they apply to your own individual status. The professional opinions that you will obtain from your accountant, attorney and banker should produce the right answers.

Counsel's advice should also be sought as to whether title to the property purchased should be in one name, joint names, corporate structure or otherwise. Discuss at length the advantages and disadvantages of the various alternatives.

For those of you who do not have your house in order in reference to estate planning and wills, I strongly urge that you do so immediately, before, if possible, or soon after your purchase of real estate. Enormous, costly and frustrating problems are present in the event of death of one of the property owners where there is no will. There is no time like the present to discuss this with your attorney —the procedure is rather simple and painless.

It is generally normal procedure for most banking institutions to require both husband and wife to execute the obligation of a mortgage, even though the title to the property may rest individually with either one or the other. This bank policy tends to eliminate sticky complications in the event of death of either one of the parties involved.

If it is your decision to purchase property in a corporate name in which you are a principal, expect the banking institution extending the mortgage to require that you personally guarantee the terms of that mortgage in addition to the corporate obligation. There are, of course, exceptions to this rule but most banking institutions in rural areas look to the individuals involved as much as they rely upon the value of their security.

Young couples who want to make country purchase, but don't have the financial wherewithal or credit experience to obtain the mortgage required, might consider having their parents agree to guarantee the obligation and at the same time place their names as part owners of the property. This might be done with the understanding that the parents would transfer their interest in the property to their children upon all or part payment of the mortgage.

The purchase of real property by a group of related or nonrelated individuals does not present any unusual financing problems. Each individual involved with the purchase must submit to the bank the same information as would be required if one were purchasing. Most financial institutions look favorably to a joint purchase as the responsibility and risk are not limited to one family. (See Chapter 16, "We'll Buy It Together.")

One of the primary concerns in the financial planning of purchase of real estate should entail what the possibilities are of resale in the event of catastrophe, unemployment, ill health, or relocation. The ability to liquidate quickly without substantial loss enhances the overall value of the property involved. Do not conclude that the property is readily salable simply because you were granted a substantial mortgage. A thorough investigation of the commercial market, economic conditions, current supply and demand ratio, environmental growth, general appeal and many other factors must be considered in projecting the resale possibilities. Your own personal decision to purchase one specific parcel does not necessarily mean that your opinions represent a good cross section of potential buyers. (Please don't think I'm trying to imply you have bad taste—it is more likely to be the contrary—you sought the unique and unusual.) The "way out" type of property might offer a much better possibility of profit at the time of resale compared to the "run-of-the-mill" parcel, but finding the right buyer is another story.

Human nature loves a bargain. Every purchaser would like to feel that what he bought was a great buy. I often wonder how many mothers and daughters run to the jewelers the morning after the engagement party to reassure themselves that they got the real thing. If your Doubting Thomas complex must be satisfied, to give you the peace of mind needed and assurance you did the right thing, spend a few dollars more and do the following: retain the most reputable and professional real estate appraiser in the area of your contemplated purchase. Ask him to forward to you an opinion of the value of the property in accordance with generally accepted standards in making appraisals in that area. The cost for such an expert opinion will be contingent upon the price of the parcel and the extent of detail you request. For an invest-

ment of two hundred dollars or less you may, or may not, rest easier.

It is not beyond the realm of possibility that soon after making your country property purchase and completion of favorable improvements an opportunity might knock at your door to make a handsome profit on an immediate resale. This very frustrating dilemma has been a frequent occurrence with the increased demand for "a country place" and to those purchasers who "saw things as they *could* be and said, why not?" Before "crying all the way to the bank" with your unexpected windfall, give consideration to the following:

1. How much income tax will be involved in the sale?
2. What are the possibilities of finding another satisfactory country place, considering the constant rise in market prices?
3. How much personal effort and labor were involved in

the improvements? (Not deductible in considering gains.)

4. Will the property be worth more, or less, in future years?

If you are the recipient of what appears to be a very attractive offer and are anticipating purchasing a larger complex with the proceeds, then accept the offer legally, contingent upon your successful purchase of another property of your choice within a specified period of time. This method will assure you of a buyer, on one hand, while you explore the possibility of finding a satisfactory replacement of property on the other.

The purchase of real estate represents for most families the largest single investment they will make. Man has for years fought for the land, worked for it, and died for it. Financing the transaction is surrounded by many technicalities and what appear to be confusing complications. But competent attorneys, bankers and brokers, working together with you, will make this process painless and simple.

6

A SOUND INVESTMENT

Probe the earth and see where your main roots run.

HENRY DAVID THOREAU

Although this book was not written to stimulate the sale of country property, I would be remiss if I did not discuss what the purchase of country property as a good investment entails. Of course, a formal appraisal of real estate is contingent upon future events—but, as the future is very unpredictable during these trying times, one cannot forecast tomorrow with any real degree of accuracy or certainty.

Just as the diamond engagement ring has symbolized love (and a good investment) for couples since time immemorial, so today these same couples label their purchase of country property as a haven of joy, as well as a sound

44

investment. I must agree with them. But don't consider that I'm endorsing what some prophets claim off the top of their heads today—"A country home with some acreage costing $45,000 now will have a market value of $100,000 in ten years or less!"

If I personally were confident of this projection of the future, I wouldn't be writing this book. I'd simply purchase a substantial number of these country properties, go to Puerto Rico or the Islands, and bask in the sun, returning in ten years to cash in my many chips.

Long-term stability and reasonable growth are the conservative reasons for making any investment. The purchase of country property is no exception. Although the final evaluation rests with you, let me elaborate upon the many factors that will generally influence the stability and growth of your investment in country property.

Land is a great natural resource that once consumed, or used for a particular purpose, is no longer available to other purposes, nor can it be manufactured. Demands for land are continually growing with a population that's expected to reach one billion people in the next seventy years. Think of the vast areas of land that have been allocated during your lifetime for hospitals, colleges, schools, universities, roads, office complexes, shopping centers, factories, motels, homes, apartments, condominiums, golf courses, race tracks, airports and a hundred other uses. The list is steadily growing. The utopian city planners have been trying for over half a century with varied success to establish untold numbers of small communities in order to reduce pressure upon the cities.

The two-home family, one in the city and one in the country, is becoming as much a part of the American way of life as the two-car garage with the two cars. Millions are migrating from the cities to such recreational, leisure and retirement areas as, for example, Vermont, Colorado, Florida, Arizona and California. Desirable land, and even not so desirable land, is rapidly becoming very expensive and very difficult to obtain. The basic law of supply and demand is having its effect, and certain repercussions will follow.

Strong and powerful conservationist factions are acting to preserve great areas of our country from being exploited. Thus, an acre of land with its blades of grass could very well become as valuable as any precious stone.

The cost of new building is spiraling daily and has become almost prohibitive; therefore demand for established property with spacious rooms and acreage at far below present-day replacement costs is on the increase.

High-speed, rapid rail transportation, helicopter type passenger aircraft, hydrofoil and massive seaplanes will soon be shuttling vast numbers of commuters daily from the overpopulated cities and their places of employment, to country homes in a matter of minutes. To live with clean air, clean water and space will be every man's goal. No personal inconvenience will be too great to achieve this end.

The trends described are but a few that will have an overwhelming effect on the stability and growth of investment value in land and country property. Unless there should be a general economic collapse, it appears evident that an investment in America's land and country property does not carry with it abnormal nor even speculative risks.

7

PROVIDE FOR CLOSING COSTS

The term *closing costs* covers those expenditures that will be made the day you take title to your property. These funds are in addition to the monies needed to pay the seller the contract price of the property.

If you are purchasing a house for $25,000, and you have obtained a commitment from the lending institution of a mortgage in the amount of $20,000, you will have to have $5,000 in cash or a certified check in hand on the day of the closing. In addition, there will be additional costs dependent upon the area of the country and the size of the transaction. Make inquiry of your broker and attorney as to your own personal commitments well before the closing date.

Many embarrassing moments have occurred around the closing table when the purchaser discovered all the "extra monies" involved at that very late date. There are closing costs in every real estate transaction, and they should be considered in the earliest stages of the big decision, when you're determining the total funds available for the purchase of property.

Most financial institutions require the borrower to pay monthly into an escrow fund a sum in addition to their regular monthly payment of principal and interest. This represents one-twelfth of the total property tax together with school taxes and insurance. The obligation to pay all property and school taxes, fire and liability insurance, when due, rests with the financial institution. These expenditures come due at various times throughout the year. The lending institution will usually require that a six-months advance be paid into the escrow fund at the time of closing.

Any taxes paid by the seller that cover any period beyond the closing date will be additional items of payment you will have to make at closing time. This sum will represent the amount computed from the day of closing. When you reimburse the seller for the pro rata taxes he has paid beyond the closing date, it is as if you had paid the taxes directly yourself.

All legal fees due your attorney, and the fees charged by the attorney representing the lending institution, are due at the time of closing. Don't be shy about asking, "How much?" all along the line.

The cost of title insurance and any land surveys you have had undertaken will also be due at the time of closing. The cost of title insurance is paid only once, an amount computed on the basis of the total purchase price of your property. Also find out from your attorney, who will order your insurance policy in advance, what the cost will be,

so that you are prepared for this expenditure as well as the others.

Many states have in effect what is known as a mortgage tax, the amount varying from state to state. This tax is paid only once and is computed on a rate per thousand dollars of each thousand dollars of mortgage obtained.

Average closing costs also include recording all legal documents, maps and other recordable instruments involved in the transaction, plus any other miscellaneous taxes that may be owed.

It is also customary procedure for the purchaser to pay the seller at the time of closing for supplies of fuel oil, coal, wood, and so forth on hand. Guess estimates are eliminated about the amount of fuel oil on hand at the time of closing by having the fuel company fill the tank to capacity that day. The bill for that amount is the obligation of the seller, and you will then reimburse him for the full tank. Deposits for the power company and telephone company may be required at this time, to continue these services without interruption.

Except for those items specified "payable by certified check only," most closing costs may be made by personal check. Your attorney and broker should advise you in advance of these details. Bring a generous supply of personal checks with you so you're not caught short by some small unexpected item of expenditure.

Your attorney or the attorney representing the lending institution will give you an itemized accounting of all the costs involved in the closing. This summary should be retained by you as a matter of record, to say nothing of income-tax purposes. Many of these items are deductible on your federal and state returns for the current year. There's a happy note!

8

COUNTRY
PROPERTY TAXES

The best investment you can make today is in taxes. They are sure to go up! A major concern in acquiring country property is the cost of all real estate and school taxes. Special tax assessments by local villages, towns and counties, in addition to the normal real estate and school taxes assessed in accordance with property value, must also be considered. Simply stated, "What are the taxes at present, and what may I expect them to be after purchase?"

Rehearse this question well before making your final decision. The answer usually will be ambiguous. Let me explain why. The system of taxing rural properties is as antiquated as the horse-drawn carriage. Property now being offered for sale that has been in the same family ownership for two or three generations or more reflects the value of many years ago. Tax rates generally have steadily increased, but assessments on this type of property have rarely changed. Local tax assessors living in the community are bound by many political and friendship ties. Sophisticated reassessment procedures performed by impartial experts have not been widely accepted by them, by reason of cost, and independent thinking.

The one-hundred-acre farm with buildings thereon might now be carrying an assessment based upon 40 percent of its present-day market value. You are informed that the total taxes for the current year are in the amount of five hundred dollars. Naturally, your first reaction is extremely favorable. If you liked the property before hearing this, you're now in love with it. Local tax assessors are advised from various legal documents recorded at the time of sale as to exactly what you paid for the property. This current value now becomes the basis for a new assessment effective with the next taxable year. Your tax bill now might be double or triple the old amount and your blood pressure could rise accordingly. The hills begin to echo with the old refrain, "Why didn't someone tell me about this before?"

Now that you have been forewarned, what is there to do about it? If the property you have purchased has changed hands within the past five years, cool it! It's not likely there will be much change as the assessment will already reflect current value. But if you feel there will be reassessment and that the tax bite could be tremendous, the following procedure could be most rewarding.

Arrange an appointment with the chairman of the local board of assessors and his committee at *their* convenience. Advise this honorable body of your intention to purchase the Jones place, and of the amount you anticipate having to pay. Inform them that you have been advised of the present tax rate, and are satisfied with the obviously fair and equitable job they are doing. Let the board know that you and your family are anxious to become an integral part of the community. Further, request a reasonable estimate of what you may expect your real estate taxes to be, based upon the proposed purchase price, and let them understand that your decision to buy will be contingent upon their reply. This meeting will give you an indication of what to expect. The personal, human element involved is bound to be more favorable than leaving the process to a routine, mechanical evaluation. Don't expect their estimate to be reduced to writing at that moment, as this is not done until their conclusions are formally entered into the books of record.

This procedure outlined might be undertaken by your local attorney, but it is suggested you consult him on this matter as to his opinion. Negotiations with the local board of assessors will be more favorable with you, or your attorney, depending upon the personalities involved.

Assuming you complete purchase, and then are not satisfied with the new tax bills, you may have recourse to the courts.

You should also inquire as to whether any major improvements are being planned within the local taxing authority area as these, too, can have a definite effect on your future taxes. Many states are now enacting legislation to eliminate inequities in assessments as well as antiquated methods of making them. The process of change in rural communities is slow. You will have to abide by country procedures, if you want to live in the country.

9

DO YOU
HAVE ZONING?

"This farm has been in our family for five generations, and I'm not about to have some fast-talking, highly paid planning expert tell *me* what I'm going to do with my land, and what I can use it for! This is the U.S.A. and *not* Russia, and all of us here at the meeting tonight are going to fight tooth and nail against this fancy zoning ordinance!"

This is a typical statement resounding in every grange hall, fire house and town hall throughout rural America. It is this type of opposition and thinking that local legislative boards, conscious of the importance of zoning, are confronted with in their efforts to pass a reasonable amount of zoning regulations.

Progress is being made, but it is most difficult and very slow. Long-established residents of country areas are adopting a self-discipline type of zoning regulated only by their conscience and good judgment.

Don't expect to find in rural areas sophisticated zoning,

as you know it in and around metropolitan areas. **The lack of zoning and strict land-use regulations should be of great concern to you in buying rural property.**

Most people leaving the city outline in great detail the type of environment they are seeking. In the majority of cases it becomes virtually impossible to fulfill the requirements without owning all the land in front, side, rear and across the road from the selected property. The properties that do offer this type of protection are becoming extinct and extremely expensive.

The next step, of course, is compromise. The obvious deterrents or minus signs in the immediate vicinity will be apparent and not worthy of space here. It is important your attention be called to environmental conditions that you normally would not be aware of which could have a serious effect upon your comfort, peace and the future value of your investment.

Physical inspection and inquiry should be made about the existence of nearby sanitary land fills (sophisticated garbage disposal areas), sewage depots, refuse dumps, junk yards, car depots, quarries in blasting operations, and the like. The presence of these things presents innumerable problems, even though they are located at a distance of a quarter of a mile away. Active recreational centers, race-tracks, amusement parks attract hordes of people, traffic and noise.

Mobile-home courts that are not subject to strict health and other essential regulations present many problems. Poorly managed dairy, poultry, horse and swine farms are great subjects for a Currier and Ives type print, but unbearable as neighbors on a hot summer day with a wind from the south!

Factories, large or small, or farm processing mills are great for the local economy, but not for your ulcers. Local town or village public works garages serve their purpose well, except when the trucks start rolling past your bedroom window at four o'clock on a summer morning. Railroad tracks are great for trains, and are also sometimes found just behind that beautiful grove of pine trees just below your pre-Revolutionary home. "Don't be concerned about that track," the owner says. "Only one train goes by every third Tuesday, provided it isn't raining." Memo to yourself. Check the weather bureau and also the railroad schedule.

I have called your attention to some of the more common unknown happenings where zoning is a dirty word. The list could be endless, but I hope it has made you aware of the fact that **you should spend a substantial amount of time investigating the surrounding countryside before you make any firm commitments.** Don't hesitate to talk to everyone you meet in the country. They all have a warehouse of information that is available even without request.

You will find in the majority of rural areas today good regulations and protection against the major problems, such as junk yards, but progress is slow. Maybe you can give the protectors a helping hand.

10

SHOULD WE
RENT FIRST?

Before you join the millions of second-home owners of this country, you might want to consider a trial run of country living. Especially if you haven't decided on any specific area, or how large an investment you can handle, renting or leasing a country house is heartily recommended.

In selecting a country home, the average couple should ideally try to set aside sufficient time to find what would be just right for them. Many purchases are made under stress and pressure, with later regrets. Desirable properties in the popular price range are becoming difficult to find in many areas of the country. Prospective purchasers make snap decisions and compromises in fear of losing what appears to be a good opportunity.

One of the key advantages to renting prior to purchase is the leisurely approach to finding the "right place." A family might discover that the country way of life is not

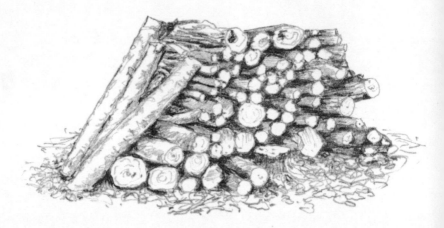

their cup of tea and forget the whole deal, thus avoiding costly mistakes. It is also possible that the rented home might be available for purchase if the mood is right. You might consider taking an "option to buy" at the time the lease is negotiated. Renting a country house will allow you to become a better informed and more sophisticated buyer.

It is sometimes difficult and in many areas impossible to rent or lease a comfortable dwelling. The available homes are either inadequate or plush and expensive. "Seek and ye shall find," but it won't be easy.

Few of the desirable places for rent are listed with real estate brokers or advertised in the newspapers, simply because the owners don't have to rely on these channels to find favorable occupants. A personal meeting with local bankers, insurance brokers, or attorneys may help you in obtaining leads on rentals of this type.

You might rent a summer or winter cottage, spend a week or two in a family type motel, and use these as a base for your scouting operations. If at all possible, spend several days in the area you have selected. It is really the first giant step you should take in your journey to the countryside.

Relax! You're coming to the country to reduce the pressures on you. Don't bring them with you on a one-day, frantic road trip.

11

WOULD YOU LIKE TO
SEE THE HOUSE?

The emphasis is on the land. The acreage is perfect, the view is magnificent. The rippling brook is more than you ever dreamed of finding. The house has character and at least three bedrooms. In fact, the whole place will lend itself to redecorating. Solid comfort will be found here.

Poetic and pleasing, but now I am going to accompany you on a tour of the house that may turn out to be your new home. This is an imaginary tour so that you can take mental notes to put in your Book of Pitfalls.

It is important that a good, warm relationship exist between you and the owner of the property. Thus, you will most likely be accompanied by your real estate broker or his representative: make it a point to keep the prearranged appointment *on time*. You should treat the seller's home and his feelings with the same kindness and consideration you show your own home. Make every effort to clear your shoes of mud and debris, and hold the young children with you by the hand.

There is a natural tendency to comment unfavorably about various obvious defects. Try to refrain from making derogatory remarks to the owners or even to the agent, if the owners are present. A warm burst of enthusiasm about a room, fireplace, or kitchen will not increase the asking price, but could act as a stimulant to the owner to give that little something extra in the transaction.

A professional real estate agency usually advises the owners not to accompany the interested purchaser on a tour of the home, but many times this advice falls on deaf ears. If the owners are present, they are usually anxious to show the amount of closet and cupboard space the house has and are not overly sensitive to your inspection. Friendly small talk does lead invariably to some valuable bits of information, and should be encouraged.

Avoid completely any reference to the selling price or other financial terms! This should be left entirely up to your agent and attorney in dealing with the seller. Direct negotiations and discussions about money at this time usually result in misunderstandings and even antagonism. All inquiries regarding the mechanical and structural condition of the home should be directed to your agent, after the tour.

Prior to or after the inspection, common courtesy dictates that you personally thank the owners for allowing you the opportunity to see their home. Discretion, diplomacy and tact should govern your remarks and attitude during the visit, as there are many reasons for putting a home on the market, not all of them happy ones. There could have been a recent death in the family, a divorce in the offing or bankruptcy. The sale could be involuntary, in many cases a sad and absolute necessity.

Now, to get back to the tour, and the physical condition of the house. Attention should be directed to any water marks or discolorations on the walls and ceilings which might indicate a roof or gutter leak problem. A reasonable explanation of the leak, that a new roof or repairs are in the offing, or have been done, and that the owners just haven't had time to redecorate since the damage should be accepted.

Turning the faucets on in the kitchen and bathrooms, flushing lavatories, will indicate the amount of water pressure, color of the water and how well the drainage system is functioning. Doors to rooms all over the house that do not close properly, windows that do not open and close freely, floors that do not appear level, major cracks in ceilings and walls are all signs warning of major structural problems in the roof, wall joints or foundation.

Inspection of the attic will provide information as to the extent of insulation, if any, roof leaks, if any, as well as the housekeeping habits of the owner.

You will find many fireplaces of great beauty that have been permanently closed or are not operating for one reason or another, including removal of the chimney. Many tales have been told about the first night spent in a new country home, the ceremonial lighting of the logs in the fireplace, and the host's dismay as smoke pours through the house, guests gasping at windows flung open; not only no chimney, but the flue had been sealed up fifty years ago.

The trip to the basement or cellar is not always the most glamorous part of your journey, but here is where

you'll find the skeletons of problems, past, present and future. Large cracks in the foundations, irregular walls, concrete, steel or wooden braces against walls all indicate major structural faults in the foundation. Inspect the entire cellar area and all rooms within; it's a good idea to come equipped with a flashlight for this area of your inspection. A dry cellar is a blessing but a rare find in most country homes, depending upon the time of year of your visit. If the main dwelling is subject to severe water problems, you will undoubtedly find an apparatus known as a sump pump in one corner of the foundation or in the center of the cellar. The purpose of the sump pump is to remove water that accumulates underneath or through the sides of the foundation. These pumps automatically start when the water reaches a certain level, pumping the water out of the basement into drainage pipes or to the surface of the land surrounding the building. They serve the purpose well and are not cause for great alarm. However, they do indicate a water problem that may be the result of a multitude of conditions, from poor drainage to poor construction. Many such troubles can be corrected by having drainage ditches dug on the outside of the foundation, by repairing the foundation where leaks are occurring, or by installing a missing gutter system to carry roof water away from the foundation walls.

Corrective procedures are costly, and an estimate should be obtained, if you wish to prepare yourself for this problem.

The electrical control panels are usually found in the cellar, and inspection will determine whether the service is sophisticated, with a heavy input service and circuit-breaker panels, or controlled by old-fashioned fuse boxes.

The central heating system (if there is one) should be checked for a service history card that is usually attached to the main unit. This will tell you the general history of the burner and accompanying units, their age, functioning and repairs made on them in the past.

A separate door from the cellar that lets you go outdoors without going through the main house, is a great advantage. Heavy tools, outdoor chairs, tables and equipment may be stored easily in the cellar, if such a door is available. You might also want to make a game room, hobby center or additional living space, in the cellar. But remember that the condition of floors, walls, height of ceiling, and their dryness limit the amount of finishing that can be done to the cellar.

It is most important that supporting beams throughout the cellar be free of dry rot and termites. If the beams are infested, you will detect the problem by careful inspection. Everyone wants the old beams that show the sign of age and history, but if they are filled with tiny little holes and covered with fresh shavings, you have a problem. This condition is easily corrected and solved, providing advanced deterioration has not taken place. Ask your broker, or look in the yellow pages of the local phone directory, for reputable firms engaged in termite control.

The outside of the home should be reviewed for storm and screen windows. Storm windows are definite heat-saving devices and recommended for all homes in the snow country. Extensive peeling of paint on the siding indicates a moisture problem, as do rotting of sills and cornices. Front steps, back steps and porch floors should be closely inspected to determine their general condition.

These are just a few of the things to look for in touring the main residence, and should be an aid in the overall appraisal of the property. However, I strongly recommend that you engage the services of a reputable, disinterested *local* contractor to review the entire residence before you consider purchase, or going into extensive repairs. He will submit a report to you or your representative on the general physical condition of the main residence, barns or service buildings. Ask him what items need immediate attention and the approximate cost involved. The cost of this professional review usually ranges from $75 to $150.

There are various organizations throughout the country whose *sole* business is inspection of property on behalf of a prospective purchaser. They issue a very detailed and complete report with fees dependent upon the extent of inspection, running anywhere from $100 to $300 in most areas. These organizations range from excellent to poor in performance, depending upon the qualifications of their personnel. It is suggested you consult with your attorney before signing a contract with such firms as to the extent of their liability if you rely on their opinion, and what recourse, if any, you will have in the event of major problems. *Caveat emptor* also applies to country property.

12

WATER, WATER

Those of you who have lived in cities most of your lives have never had to be concerned about the source of your water. It has been simply a matter of going to the sink, bathtub or shower, and turning the knob. You probably couldn't care less where it comes from, just as long as it's there, and in abundant supply. The responsibility for furnishing your water rested with the landlord, or a public authority. It was their business, not yours.

Now that you're coming to the country, you must know the source, availability, quality and abundance of water on what will be your land, if you sign the contract. Most rural areas are not served by a public water supply, and as costs would be prohibitive will not be in the foreseeable future. **Each country unit must provide itself with its own source of water.** So its presence can no longer be taken for granted.

In the country the four main sources of this precious

commodity are drilled wells, driven wells, springs, and cisterns. A drilled well is the most sophisticated, reliable, dependable and purest source of water. Well-drilling firms perform the service with the aid of equipment designed for this specific purpose of boring through the earth and through rocks to depths ranging from an average of sixty to three hundred feet. Obtaining water through this method is a usual procedure.

A driven well means water is obtained by driving a pipe, stake or similar penetrating instrument, into the ground to obtain a supply of water near the surface, usually from a spring. Many rural areas have natural springs that allow dwellers there to get their water by placing a plastic pipe in the center of said spring, bringing the water into their dwellings by either putting a pump in the spring, or letting the water come by gravity flow alone when the spring is on higher ground than the house it is supplying.

A cistern is a large storage area for water usually constructed of brick, stone or cement, varying in size from five hundred gallons to many thousands. The source of cistern water is rain or melted snow that has fallen upon the roofs, or in catch basins, and then funneled by gutters and other contrivances into the cistern. The water is then pumped from the cistern into the main residence or other buildings.

One of the first questions that you should ask your real estate representative or seller about land that interests you is, "What's the main source of water?" Although well-established rural property most likely has a drilled well, it's not unusual to find places that do not.

A modern household depends on water in its use of automatic washing machines, dishwashers, garbage disposals, air conditioning, and bathroom facilities. Therefore, the yield in gallons per minute of a drilled well is of vital importance. **An average family will require a capacity of at least three gallons per minute, although I would be much more comfortable with six to ten gallons per minute.** The capacity of a drilled well will be certified by the well-drilling firm that performs the service. You should try to obtain a letter from them, or the previous owners, as to the well's capacity.

The local or state health department will test the water for you to determine whether or not it's pure enough for human consumption, and will issue a certificate to this effect. Most drilled wells do meet these standards. However, I suggest the test as a precaution to insure that the water supply has not been polluted or made unsafe since the last test was made. One of the most common causes of drilled-well pollution is a septic tank located too close to the water supply, so that seepage from this sewage-disposal system contaminates the well. The cost of the water test is nominal, and the test usually takes less than a week.

The driven-well source presents many risks. It may become affected by surface drainage, periods of long drought, insufficient capacity and pollution. The fact that it may have been a main water supply for the last hundred years should not impress you to the point of complete satisfaction.

Good springs do offer a refreshing source of water, but they are also subject to surface conditions, pollution and supply problems. What springs do offer is a marvelous auxiliary to the more sophisticated drilled well, thus enhancing the value of the property substantially.

The cistern type of supply is the main source of water

in many of the Caribbean Islands, where rain is the primary source of fresh water. There are also sections of the United States, particularly the desert areas, where this may also serve as the main source of water supply. Many farm and country homes use the cistern water for washing and bathroom facilities, but not for drinking, unless water purification apparatus is installed. Cisterns are subject to pollution, algae, growths and rodents.

If your country place does not have a good drilled well

that provides adequate water, then consider having one drilled. The cost is computed per foot of depth and depends upon the area and drilling conditions. A minimum of one thousand dollars should be allocated for the drilling process and various pumps and connections to same.

There is *no* definite method or means to determine how deep you will have to drill to obtain an adequate supply of water. Various areas are generally known to yield a good supply of good water; investigation of recent wells driven by neighboring owners might be indicative of what you may expect, but not necessarily conclusive.

Drilled wells in many areas produce excellent but "hard" water. Don't be surprised to find a water-softener apparatus in the cellar. It is most common and does an excellent job in softening the water before use. Many areas of the country yield what is known as "sulfur" water. This type of water meets all health standards, but you will readily detect by drinking or smelling it a sulfur or rotten-egg taste or aroma. It is a matter of extreme concern. However, there is now on the market an apparatus similar to a water softener to remove the sulfur odor.

Many of our clients anticipate installing an in-ground swimming pool and do not give any consideration to where the water is coming from to fill it. We immediately inform them that they should not tax their present water supply with the thousands of gallons of water required to fill the pool. They should contract with a firm who will fill the pool by means of a five-thousand-gallon tank truck. Most pools will reuse this supply through the season by means of a filtering system.

I have been strongly criticized by attorneys, landowners

and others, for recommending to my clients, before buying any land on which they expect to erect a home, that they do the following:

1. Enter into a contract to purchase the site selected, be it one acre or five hundred, and to purchase said site at the price agreed upon *after* having a well drilled at a reasonable depth with a minimum supply of four gallons per minute.
2. In the event that the conditions of (1) are not met, and the buyers having so performed at their own cost and expense, then they should have the right to withdraw without any further liability for the purchase of this site.

If you feel that you are part of the law of averages, which certainly will result in your having an adequate water supply, then proceed without my above suggestion. But if you find, after you have purchased the property for a substantial amount of money, you are unable to obtain a sufficient supply of water, you will wish you had taken my advice. It certainly makes good sense to invest a few thousand dollars in getting a good water supply, rather than finding yourself the owner of a $20,000 piece of land that has no water.

I suggest the same procedure be followed in the purchase of even a building lot in the country of only an acre or two. The land developer should be willing to guarantee an adequate water supply and if such is not forthcoming should refund your money as a condition of purchase. I admit that I am overly conscientious and ultraconservative, but you will remember in my opening remarks that I wanted your journey to the country to be as pleasant and trouble free as possible.

I caution you in many of these areas throughout the book because I have actually seen and experienced the sad results for those who did not look before they leaped.

13

UTILITIES

Power blackouts in major metropolitan cities over the past few years, both in summer and winter, should have made you flick your switch of interest and concern as to available power to serve your Shangri-La. The demand for sufficient voltage is ever increasing, be it in the city or the country.

Most rural areas are serviced by major power companies, but are classified as "rural service." This service varies substantially from one area to another. **Costs of installation and use may present problems, and it is most vital that you make yourself aware of the status of power in the area in which you've decided to buy.**

If you are buying an existing and established home, make inquiries as to whether the present service is capable of handling additional loads, such as more appliances, air-conditioning units, power tools and equipment. Wiring in many of the older places is totally inadequate, thus making fire insurance coverage difficult to obtain, to say nothing of the hazard to life and limb. A new, heavier service, combined with new wiring and outlets, is expensive. If you are in doubt, contact the local power company representative or an electrician for an expert opinion.

If you are anticipating building a country home on land that you have selected to buy, it is mandatory that you consider whether or not power is available to the site. The utility company in many rural areas will bring the power to your location from an existing power line free of charge, providing it does not exceed a certain distance from the main source of power, which is usually along a town road or highway or adjacent property. In the event that the site you have selected is one or two thousand feet or more from the existing source of power, you will be shocked to learn that this carrier of public utilities may charge you as much as two dollars per foot or more to supply you with electric power.

The smiling power representative will inform you that this is not a problem because they have an easy five-year "charge plan," with easy monthly installments that are added to your regular monthly bill. It is not uncommon nor unlikely for you to select the ideal spot in the woods for your chalet two to three thousand feet from the source of power. Add this expense to the cost of a newly paved, private road, the well drilling, the septic system plus the purchase price of the land, and *suddenly* the already established place, along the quiet town road, begins to look like your oasis in the desert.

Various power companies have reimbursing agreements for the costs explained above, in the event that a certain number of additional customers beyond your property

request power in the future, within a specified period of years.

Cooking in rural areas is usually accomplished with electric stoves, as natural gas is not available. If you ladies feel that your best gourmet dishes can only be done on a gas stove, then simmer down—tank bottled gas is available in most rural areas.

Before you close title to any property not presently serviced with electric power, it is suggested you obtain all the estimates on installation in writing from an officer in the power company empowered to act upon and give such information. It is not unlikely that the power company may take a substantial period of time to construct a power line to your facility.

Many recent purchasers have asked us if they should consider buying their own generator in the event of power failure. We are also asked, when service is not available or too costly to install, if generator equipment should be substituted. Power failure beyond a short period of time is not a common occurrence in most areas. Consequently, it does not justify the expense of a generator for the infrequent times it would be required.

The cost of a generating facility and the operation of

same on a full-time basis as a substitute for normal power is substantial; it is not an economically sound investment over a period of years. Many large farms and estates do have their own generator systems in combination with the main power system, used only during periods of power failure because of potential spoilage of milk, meat and other perishables.

So before you blow your fuse, talk to the power company. You will find local representatives most cooperative.

Phone service throughout these great United States is rapidly deteriorating in some aspects, and rural areas are no exception. Local phone companies vary from one area to another in service and efficiency from absolutely impossible to excellent.

The popular pastime for many country ladies is gathering all the local news and gossip on a ten-party line through conversations overheard that are endless. Just another new experience and reason for you to move to the country. You have never truly reached the point of total exasperation until you have lived with a party-line system.

It is possible, depending upon the facilities available, to have a private line, but one of the reasons you are moving to the country is to "get away from that damn telephone"! You may be assured the phone company will try to make this possible. However, we recommend that you notify your local telephone office well in advance of your closing or moving date, requesting installation and available service. Telephone service in rural areas is improving daily. (At least if we believe the advertisements of AT&T.)

14

LAKE PROPERTY

Most established properties available for purchase near or on good lakes do not allow the buyer the opportunity to acquire much acreage along with the house. Many of the homes, cottages or facilities near or on lakes were established at a time when there was a lack of overall planning or zoning.

Since lake facilities, and the properties bordering them, were usually used only during the summer season, a variety of "cottage type" buildings were erected. Many homes didn't have cellars, foundations, heating systems, insulation, good bathroom facilities, nor were they winterized. Further, many lake properties today follow the antiquated system of obtaining water directly from the lake. Many questions have arisen as to whether or not occupants have the legal right to lake use and/or lake frontage.

Extreme caution should be used in the purchase of lake

property, especially in the areas of availability of utilities, sewage disposal, water supply, and examination of title.

Owners of lake properties still using the lake as the main source of water supply have in recent years installed chlorinator systems in order to purify the water. If you are desirous of using the lake property as a year-round retreat, or home, with the lake as your main water supply, it would be wise to investigate whether or not the lake freezes during the winter.

One should also check with the local department of highways to determine if the access roads to the lake area are under public control and maintenance, particularly during the winter months where snowplowing is vital.

Control of good lake areas by owner associations, or local regulatory authorities, is of the utmost importance. You should investigate garbage disposal, public utilities, power boat control, the extent of pollution, if any, the extent of public areas and whether large public camp sites are available. As to cost, any sizable amount of acreage that might be available in the immediate vicinity of a good lake facility, or having an established residence thereon, will usually be 20 percent to 30 percent higher than comparable acreage five or ten miles away from the lake.

If you are planning to buy property near but not directly on a lake, a thorough investigation should be made to determine if you have the legal right to swimming or docking facilities. This information should be confirmed and relied upon only by advice of your attorney. Also, investigate whether anticipated activities, such as sail boating, water skiing, and motor boating, are allowed.

If you have small children, consideration should be

given to the availability of medical care, hospital facilities and the proximity of shopping facilities for groceries and other supplies.

It would certainly be wise to introduce yourself to several established owners in the area, and gather their ideas about the present and future status of the lake community.

Investigation should be made as to any large parcels of land nearby which might lend themselves to the development of recreational facilities that could cause a drain on local facilities by reason of overpopulation. This is less likely to happen in small lake areas.

There are some excellent, well-established and well-constructed homes in and around good lake areas, but we advise extreme caution and investigation before "jumping into the lake." The possibility of "drowning" in noise, population and pollution is likely. As we said before, local zoning and restrictions are either not in being, or have come too late to many areas.

There is a great demand for private lakes that range in size from ten to twenty acres, all within the confines of a property. Unless all sides of the entire lake facility are bordered by lands to be conveyed to you, problems could develop. For example, property bordering on any portion of the lake facility, even though it represents a small portion, could be sold for commercial or other undesirable use, including a multifamily dwelling. The new owners and present owners, having the right to use the lake, might disturb the tranquillity you are seeking. A thorough investigation should be made of these possibilities. Further, find out if anyone has the legal right, riparian (see Glossary) or otherwise, to use the lake for recreation or water supply. Many courts have stated that anyone having title to land bordering on a lake, stream or other type of water-course, technically owns to the center of that water facility.

Many states now have extensive regulations dealing with the use of water, control and damming of same, through the change of direction, or whatever. These regulations prohibit the freedom of use of water facilities for your own purposes.

If you have sophisticated plans for the water facility on or bordering your property, and said facility has been a major cause for the purchase of the entire property, then every phase of its use, ownership and control should be thoroughly reviewed by your attorney before closing the transaction.

It appears that water is such a vital part of our ecology today that its use and ownership may very likely become public domain in order to preserve and maintain this great natural resource. Both federal and state governments have the right to acquire private property for necessary public use by condemnation known as "eminent domain." This right is not limited to water supplies but to the taking of any property where the health and welfare of the public are involved.

If you are anticipating purchasing a private lake facility, you should retain an engineering firm to make a complete analysis of the water, the depth and condition of the bottom, whether or not it is spring fed, and its status during periods of extreme drought.

15

I'LL SUBDIVIDE SOME

"I would like a home in the country on a substantial tract of land that I can subdivide at a later date into several parcels, for sale to the public, or my friends."

This typical request and goal of many seeking country property is most worthy in theory, but in practice laden with a multitude of barriers. The most sophisticated and professional land developers in and around metropolitan areas are amazed at the number of problems involved in developing country property as opposed to suburban area projects.

It is not my intention in this chapter to direct comments to professionals, but to those of you contemplating selling more than four but fewer than ten parcels out of your original purchase. If your purchase is financially contingent upon selling a portion of your anticipated purchase within a reasonable period of time from acquisition, your plans could easily go astray.

A typical example is the young couple who literally fell in love with a pre-Revolutionary, center-hall colonial home situated on a parcel of two hundred acres. The seller would not entertain the idea of disposing of any less acreage than the entire amount. The considerable amount of acreage was a major factor reflected in the total selling price. It was considerably more than our young couple could afford to finance; the parcel contained more acreage than they thought they needed for protection, enhancement of the house or use.

Beaming happily, the young husband turned to his wife, proud of his rapid calculations. "We can swing it, dear, I have it all figured out. We'll buy the whole two hundred acres with the house, keep fifty acres around it and sell the other hundred and fifty acres. That'll make fifteen nice ten-acre parcels."

Quick figuring of anticipated revenue from the sale of the fifteen subdivisions brought them immediate joy, success—and a fountain pen to sign on the dotted line. They were now to be the proud owners of a beautiful colonial home with fifty acres paid for in full by the anticipated profits derived from the sale of their subdivision.

This typical story is being widely acted out throughout our country, but the number of happy endings are relatively few.

Let me tell you about what is on Pitfall Lane for you and Little Red Riding Hood on the way to Grandma's farm.

In many areas state, county and local governments have passed or are in the process of passing many laws and codes regulating the subdivision of lands applicable to those anticipating the sale of as few as three parcels. The more parcels to be subdivided, the thicker the rule book be-

comes. The basic provisions of the laws are aimed to provide adequate water, sewerage, roads, utilities, as well as to govern the size of the parcels themselves. The owner or subdivider must comply with various health codes, and gain written approval and acceptance from the authorities regulating the sale of these parcels before being allowed to offer the units for sale to the public. Any violation of the law is subject to stiff fines and penalties.

If your projected plans include selling any portion of your anticipated purchase, you should inquire from your attorney as to what laws are applicable in regard to your venture. Local zoning ordinances now in being, or anticipated, should be considered. The cost of engineering, mapping, installation of roads, sewerage, water and other utilities might prove to be prohibitive in proportion to anticipated profit on sale of the parcels.

There is a further possibility that the topography of the

land and nature of the soil might not be conducive to the building program of the lots' potential buyers, while the lack of public water and sewerage facilities in country areas leaves the problem of wells and sewage-disposal systems in the buyers' hands.

There are many two-hundred-acre-plus parcels of land with only enough road frontage for ingress and egress to the home already established on the property. If you don't want annoying traffic passing your front door at all hours of the day and night, private access roads are mandatory. Thus, substantial road frontage (a minimum of five hundred feet on a good primary or secondary road) should be a prime consideration in purchasing country property, whether or not you are planning to subdivide.

Offering several parcels of land for sale from your original purchase changes your real estate tax level immediately. Filing a map of the parcels offered in the local county clerk's office changes the legal nature of your total property from what was probably agricultural, to commercial. You must, therefore, further consider the possibility of paying very high real estate taxes during the period before buyers have been found for your lots.

There are also many direct and indirect costs involved in the selling of only three or four parcels of land that should be anticipated well in advance. In addition to those mentioned above, there are legal fees, utility costs, surveying bills, application fees, real estate commissions and other miscellaneous selling costs.

Let's assume that, having jumped all the hurdles, you now conclude that selling some parcels would be a worthy undertaking. If this is so, then it is strongly suggested that you set firm restrictions on the buyers, especially if your property is in an area not governed by local building codes and/or rules for property use. These restrictions would be covenants of use, that is, limits on the type of buildings to be constructed, along with other rules and regulations that would protect your remaining home property, as well as attract others to the parcels available for purchase.

In anxiety or haste to sell their first parcel or two, owners who have not put restrictions in the deeds of sale may find themselves surrounded by mobile homes, campers, horse stables, chicken coops, commercial enterprises, radio towers, recording studios and other such goodies.

If you are considering selling some of your land, think about dividing it into two or three very large parcels, rather than many small units, since the average purchaser of this type of country property today is not attracted to being part of what would be considered a "development." There are far fewer problems involved in the sale of two or three large parcels of twenty acres than in ten smaller ones. Larger lots will also afford you a better opportunity for controlling the environment. Remember the base property that you retain will be seriously affected by what surrounds it.

Don't complicate your life in the country by becoming involved in a land-subdivision project—a business that even professionals are seldom able to cope with—unless you're a speculative genius with more than a pocketful of rye!

16

WE'LL BUY IT
TOGETHER

The perfect way to end a beautiful friendship is to buy some country property in partnership with two or three of your favorite couples. Equally true, "there is strength in numbers," except when all the numbers add up to relatives banding together for the same reason. There are exceptions to every rule, so we'll be optimistic and dwell only upon the happy household of "joint purchase."

There are distinct advantages in buying large parcels of contiguous land in excess of one hundred acres by two or more individuals or families. The cost per acre for the entire parcel is much less for the pro rata share distributed to each partner than it would be for the smaller individual parcel if purchased separately on the open market. The partners involved are then in a position to control a substantial amount of their environment by working toward one interest and common goals.

The fear of undesirable activity that normally presents a

problem to the smaller acreage owner is greatly alleviated. The cost of roads, utilities, lighting, water facilities, recreational areas is shared, thus reducing the individual burden which might be economically prohibitive to one person.

Building or remodeling three or more homes simultaneously results in substantial savings in labor and materials if the project is concentrated in one area by one contractor. One of the biggest problems involved with joint purchasing of real property is the fair and equitable distribution of the acreage and facilities.

Shall we listen at the keyhole?

"You will have more road frontage."

"Your acreage has the better view."

"My children are in college and won't be here as often."

"I'm not sure whether I really have one hundred acres."

"Your section was surveyed before we bought it."

"Your acreage has a pond. I'll have to dig one."

"The beautiful trees are only on your portion."

"Why should I pay for your road? You're going to use it."

"It's not necessary to take off that asphalt shingle. Shingling is shingling and it will save heating costs."

"The Fourth of July weekend is definitely mine!"

"I don't see why we can't expand the one main house into separate apartments, instead of going to the expense of building three separate homes."

"The least you could have done last weekend was to wash the dirty dishes!"

"My wife hates it up there and says it's the worst mistake

we ever made. Of *course* I'll sell you my interest! But you know how much property has gone up since we bought it."

"If you want air conditioning in your bedroom, get it yourself. I can't stand it!"

"What happened to all the steaks we brought up last week? I don't mind if those hogs ate them, but the least they could do is replace them."

"We should each have our own liquor cabinet with our own key."

"I'm not paying for the cost of plowing the road. You know I was in Florida all winter!"

"Share the taxes equally? You know your portion is in the township that had the increase—not mine!"

"Life is too damn short to argue over something so trivial, but in this matter, you're entirely wrong!"

Not only have we listened to typical conversations but have actually opened the door to what some of the problems are in what appears to be the ideal way to purchase country property.

The success or failure of "We'll Buy It Together" rests entirely with the personality of the males, females and children involved. Make a trial run by going away on vacation with the group with whom you plan to make a joint purchase. Pool all resources and jointly outline your itinerary, side trips, meals and recreation.

A less complicated method of purchasing real property jointly is to subdivide immediately the entire original purchase in accordance with a predetermined plan whereby each participant owns his specific parcel without obligation or involvement with the others.

The purchase of a recreational type facility to be used by the partnership in accordance with a schedule of use not interfering with the others might present some problems but has proven to be fairly successful. Title to the property involved is jointly held with a written agreement setting forth conditions in the event of death or withdrawal from the partnership.

Any formal involvement with others in a joint venture exposes all those concerned to many risks, obligations and various types of liabilities. The initial concept to purchase jointly a country place may appear simple and advantageous, but the hazards are many. An attorney should be consulted before joining hands and dancing around the mulberry bush. You may be assured that your counsel will advise formal agreement setting forth in detail the respective rights and obligations of all those concerned with each phase of the purchase, its use, improvements, resale of all or part, individual personal liability, estate involvement, financing and decision-making policies.

Our files contain the histories of hundreds of joint-purchase prospective clients who initially started their search for country property with every good and honorable intention. But along the grueling way of noncompromise and disagreement, the decision was reached to go it alone and live happily ever after.

17

BUILDING OR
REBUILDING
IN THE COUNTRY

"My brother-in-law, the dentist, he bought this great big old barn last year that was about ready to collapse, right in the middle of an open field of ten acres, and you should see what he has now!"

I didn't ask and she didn't tell me. But let me tell *you* what he has now. A double hernia, an overdrawn bank account, and divorce papers from his wife!

The *before* and *after* pictures of remodeled country property that frequently appear in *House Beautiful* and *Better Homes and Gardens* are enough to make any red-blooded American male reach for the nearest hammer and saw, plus a road map to the fields of clover. What does it really take besides a roll of film between *before* and *after*? Only $100,000, a prescription for ulcers and a weekly appointment with your psychiatrist. If you think for one moment I'm trying to discourage you, you're right!

If you are entertaining any ideas of a building program in the country, be it do-it-yourself, or by professionals, the

problems you will experience with any type of major construction in the country are very similar to those connected with building industries in the city. A serious shortage of good painters, carpenters, masons, electricians, plumbers and laborers exists nationwide. Substantial contractors are concentrating their efforts on building apartment complexes, office buildings and government facilities. The individual, custom contract builder no longer finds it profitable or practical to offer this service to the individual public. A shortage of labor, technicians and subcontractors is rapidly making the one home custom builder extinct. Spiraling costs of labor and materials have discouraged the building of custom homes, or substantial additions.

Many banking institutions will not give firm mortgage commitments until the anticipated work to be performed has been completed. This is especially true in instances where the purchaser is buying country property that needs many improvements and does not have the basic utility requirements that satisfy bank policy. Simply stated, this means that all of your available cash might be allocated for the down payment and closing costs, leaving very little on hand to pay for the major improvements.

This section of our visit is directed to those of you who anticipate buying country land, and building exactly the type of home or vacation dwelling you feel best suits your needs. The purchase of land is a rather simple process and without complications, providing you follow the suggestions outlined in other sections of this book.

If you or members of your immediate family have not been involved in any building projects during the past two years, you will be completely astounded, shocked and dismayed at the cost involved in the construction of the most modest home, chalet or room addition, to say nothing of mere improvements. It is true, however, that we in country areas are fortunate to have the independent carpenter, cabinet-maker and combination handyman whose generation is rapidly disappearing. These are the men from yesterday who never lost their pride in workmanship, and who are still to be found in many small communities.

As an alternative to custom building, there are the many packaged home deals available to the lot or landowner. These homes are mass-produced in factories and are composed of factory-finished units that can be transported to a site by truck, and installed by means of cranes and other mechanical methods. The advertised packaged price is always extremely attractive. However, investigate thoroughly before saying and signing "I do!" Don't become obligated until your attorney reviews the entire contract and advises you what the package really includes. The cost of transportation, foundation, well, heating, electrical and plumbing system, septic system, painting, appliances and dozens of other items required for the finished product may or may not be included in the package.

Whatever the building project you mean to undertake, first inquire of your local attorney, or bank, about the reliability of the firm or contractor you intend to use. An entire book could be written on the hazards involved in any major building undertaking. By employing a contractor or firm with a proven record of honesty, dependability and performance, 95 percent of all these hazards can be avoided.

Your contract estimate may be substantially lower from the unknown fly-by-night, but the net result could be lawsuits, disappointments and inferior workmanship. Do not become involved in any down payments or agreements of any kind without the advice of local counsel. Beware of off-the-cuff estimates, especially if these estimates are a determining factor in the selection of an established property, or future purchase of land for new building.

Remodeling or improving of old country homes involves a great deal more than what simply appears on the surface. The entire heating, plumbing and electrical system may be difficult to change without major unexpected costs. Many walls and ceilings in the older homes have two or three layers of brick or plaster which might make the costs of the anticipated remodeling prohibitive. It would be impossible to state rule-of-thumb building or remodeling costs throughout the United States today with any real degree of accuracy. Too many variable factors are involved, such as materials used, local labor rates, extent of frills and extras. Good judgment dictates that you obtain at least two estimates for each job to be contracted for, discuss these estimates with a bank officer in your country community and get his opinion as to whether or not these prices are in accordance with local rates. If a building program is part of your immediate future plans, investigate thoroughly *before* purchasing your country property.

There is an overwhelming demand for old country schoolhouses, abandoned churches, barns, mills and silos, the idea in the mind of the buyer being to remodel these buildings into unique or quaint homes. The goal is an admirable one, and results have been breathtaking. If this is your "thing," lots of luck! But for the sake of being practical, anticipate all costs by obtaining written estimates for work to be performed before taking title to the next feature article in *House Beautiful*.

18

I WANT TO
TILL THE SOIL!

Many years ago everyone was humming, whistling or singing the refrain, "How're you gonna keep 'em down on the farm!" Over the past few years letters and calls have been pouring in to every brokerage firm throughout the United States from people with every type of background *but* farming wanting to purchase a fruit, vegetable, poultry or dairy farm. They all reflect the movement back to the land and tilling the soil.

This American Dream can rapidly become an American Nightmare for most of those who are not in an outside 70 percent tax bracket! Your chances of making any money and not going broke within the first three years in most farming operations are much better at the roulette tables in Las Vegas than they are trying to dig a living out of the soil. The capital required for raw land, buildings, equipment and operating costs for what would be classified as just a small farm is astronomical.

A good herd of one hundred milking cows, which is a minimum in dairy-farm operation today, means an investment of $40,000. To support this type of farm operation you need three hundred acres of good tillable land for crops and pasture. A minimum of $100,000 to $150,000 would be required for the purchase of land, if available. Equipment to maintain the operation would run $40,000 to $60,000 in additional funds. Quick computation of these few basic costs brings us to a $200,000 investment without sophisticated buildings, silos, residence, working capital and homes for farm help. The profit margin is unbelievably low. The volume produced by the one hundred head of cattle would not begin to amortize the direct and indirect costs involved.

This simple example pertaining to a dairy farm is applicable to fruit, poultry and vegetable operations in proportion. The cost of production is so far out of proportion to prices farmers obtain for their produce that it is ridiculous. The discouraging remarks included in this chapter are directed to those of you with less than $75,000 of capital who are thinking about transplanting yourselves and your families from the city to a working farm.

Farm families who have been operating over the past three or four generations are just about surviving and eking out a living. This is true where their farms are paid for and they do not have heavy mortgages, obligations and other debts. The average city person has never had the slightest conception of how difficult his country cousin has had it in trying to survive and make a living from the soil. In addition to all of the normal problems an average farmer has to cope with, he must face whims of nature that are completely uncontrollable and unpredictable,

and have a direct effect on whether or not he makes the grade. Thousands of dreams and hopes have literally gone up in smoke during periods of drought, floods, hailstorms, tornadoes, fires, blight, disease or late-season freeze.

You ask, "Why do they stay?" The answer is not a simple one. In many cases they have no other choice but to be optimistic and hope the next year may be better. They're so deeply involved they can't get out—just waiting for Providence to tell them, "You may take six giant steps forward." I have witnessed many farmers going deeply into debt three bad years in a row with the fourth year being just good enough to liquidate some of the obligations of the previous three years, then starting the whole mad cycle all over again.

Many genuine farmers may be compared to artists. They love and enjoy what they are turning out, creating from scratch, with a feeling for form and effect. The production of their particular crop is their "thing." Stop to think for a moment that most farmers may be likened to manufacturers. However, in contrast to the manufacturer, they produce a product from seed to package. In most cases they do not know what they will receive for their finished product until some wholesaler or cooperative sends them a check after deducting the dozens of costs involved in marketing.

Ask the average farmer how things are and his usual reply will be, "I'm so busy that I don't have time to go to the bank to borrow money to pay for my last month's bills." The plight of the average small farmer is extremely sad. He represents a hard core of rural America, extremely independent by nature, who has refused for the most part to accept the union principle of collective bargaining or organization to improve his status. The only thing that two farmers will agree upon is what the third one is doing wrong in operating his farm. The farmer has been a victim of many circumstances. One of the biggest problems has been his dependence upon someone else, middleman or otherwise, to market his product.

The cost of producing a good box of apples today is a

minimum of three dollars, under the most advanced and ideal conditions. This three dollars represents the cost of labor, materials, supplies, storage, handling, etc. It is not uncommon for a farmer to receive as little as one dollar for every box of apples produced.

Many farmers today are finding that their land is worth more for industrial, development and recreational purposes than for farming. Thousands of small farms are being liquidated each year. The only bright star on the horizon after generations of blood, sweat and tears is that they are receiving very substantial sums for their land and buildings.

Huge farm complexes are extremely attractive properties to those wishing to be near the soil and simultaneously to have favorable tax write-offs. Many of these tax benefits available to those with large nonfarming incomes are being eliminated by changes in legislation in both federal and state tax laws. The "hobby" farmer is going to have a difficult time deducting his losses in accordance with the current tax laws and the Internal Revenue Service.

Naturally, those who are genuinely involved in the operation of a major agricultural endeavor will be given every consideration, providing it is well established that their motives are for profit. I strongly advise anyone with substantial capital and high earnings to discuss the tax benefits available to him under present Internal Revenue laws with his tax attorney or accountant. Many large farming operations are making money and offer attractive tax shelters in depreciation and other write-offs.

Personally, I was born and raised on a small farm in upstate New York, witnessed and was part of years of heartbreak and back break while my family tried to survive from a diversified farm of vegetables, fruit, and dairy cattle. Yes, a farm is a great place for children to develop a sense of values and responsibilities, as well as a healthy mind and body, but the economic results can be cruel, uncontrollable and impossible to comprehend. It is not easy to appreciate the beautiful sunset on a July evening after it has rained for five consecutive days, leaving the entire raspberry crop, representing a year's work, "a-molderin' in the ground." The fragrance of new-mown hay is not the topic of conversation after a sixty-mile-an-hour wind and hailstorm has hit the area, smashing and scattering hundreds of boxes of ready-to-pick apples. The greatest lesson that one can learn in growing up on a farm is compassion for everyone who has tried to make a living on an average small farm.

It is true that today the physical effort expended by the farm operator and his family is small compared to a generation or two ago. The variety of modern types of farm machinery available today has eliminated some physical labor, and brought about greater efficiency. The law of diminishing returns still applies, however, as the income generated by the average small farm usually does not justify the tremendous expenditures this type of modern machinery demands.

I have talked with hundreds of engineers, architects, stock brokers, attorneys and businessmen over the past few years who had the yearning to buy a working farm but did not have the slightest background in the problems they were to face. Most of them listened. The few who blithely made the move anyway are with few exceptions in serious financial trouble after only a short time of operating their farms. Their one satisfaction is that land values have increased sufficiently to the point where their farms can be liquidated at a greater market price than at purchase, equaling their initial investment and accumulated losses.

A great deal has been said about government subsidies but most of these programs are not geared for nor applicable to the operation of the average small farm.

The immediate future does not look bright for the small farm owner. The large farm complexes will become larger. The medium to small farms will collapse, or be sold at ever increasing prices as the demand for land continues to be greater than the supply.

19

PONDS

"Your own pond!" Everyone is looking for his own pond with as much zest as Diogenes looked for the honest man. I don't know if Diogenes found him, but it is possible for you to find the right kind of pond, even though it won't be easy!

What may appear in March or April, after the spring rains or melting snows, to be a pool of great delight, could resemble an eighth-hole sand trap in July and August. You then have to call up all your friends and tell them to forget their bikinis and bring their nine irons. I would also venture to say there have been thousands of overflowing septic tanks admired by the innocent as great watersheds for fun and games for the family and friends.

Most advertisements for typical country properties claim "excellent pond sites available." This may or may not be true, depending upon the basic requirements of a good pond for swimming and fishing.

If the property has an existing pond, and you wish to utilize it for more than mere beauty, you must determine:

1. If the source of water is of a permanent type, such as a good stream that does not disappear in the drought of summer, or a natural spring near, or contained within, the pond.
2. The size and depth of the facility. A good swimming pond should be at least ten feet deep at the center.
3. The type of soil or composition of the sides and bottom of the pond, information of vital importance in swimming, unless muddy feet are your "thing."
4. If there is adequate overflow facility for continuous fresh water, and circulation.
5. Is the pond stocked with fish? If the answer is affirmative, a good supply of fresh water is indicated.

Circulation and flow are important because stagnant ponds are breeding grounds for mosquitoes and other undesirable insects, can become thick with algae, and may give off unpleasant odors.

In some localities, any water facility over four acres is called a lake. It is wise to determine in advance the size of the claimed pond or lake before driving many miles out in the country in response to an advertisement.

Through various local, state and federal agencies, many areas offer free advice and guidance on the status of a pond or small lake and the feasibility of expanding it. Take advantage of this type of counsel, for the people involved know what they're talking about, and can offer you an abundance of information based on experience. Various health departments are also available for testing the quality of the water, and will advise you if swimming in the pond meets with their approved standards.

If your pond is not stocked, contact your local state

conservation office. In almost any state they will be happy
to supply you with a variety of fish at no cost, providing
your water facility will sustain them.

Thousands of ponds and lakes have been created
throughout our country over the past few years. There are
numerous state and federal agencies, such as the Department of Agriculture, State Conservation Department,

Water Resources Bureau, ready, willing and most able to assist you with your undertaking. Costs vary, depending upon the area involved, the location selected, the availability of natural supply of water, size of the lake or pond desired and excavation problems involved.

It is recommended that you retain an engineer to give you detailed guidance and work with these agencies on your plans. Don't rely upon a lay opinion. Reasonable estimates as to proposed costs are available before any major obligation is incurred.

A good pond or small lake on the property enhances the overall value of your country home substantially. It will prove to be a great private recreational asset, if you are able to fish in the spring and fall, swim in the summer and hold skating parties in the winter.

A word of caution to those having young children. Give consideration to permanently fencing in the entire area surrounding the pond or lake for reasons that are obvious. Another good reason for fencing is to eliminate a very serious hazard to those snowmobiling during the winter when a few inches of snow will camouflage the water area which might not be completely frozen over.

A pond or small lake *may be* a thing of beauty, and a joy forever, but check it out!

20

CUSTOMS
COUNTRY STYLE

Country folk, like city folk, have their idiosyncrasies and wayward winds. I have been very proud of the thousands of city inhabitants whom I've introduced to my fellow country men, because of the ease with which they've settled into the country way of life. Let me tear a few pages out of the unwritten book of country protocol and share them with you.

Introduce yourself to the officers of the local bank in your country community right away. Open a nominal checking account, or savings, or both. If you wish to establish credit in a community, be prepared to submit a statement of your financial condition to the bank. This new relationship will provide many personal benefits, as well as giving you a convenient local banking facility, besides providing you with an on-the-spot reference for local tradesmen, suppliers and others who might be reluctant otherwise to issue immediate short- or long-term credit.

Besides you will find that in most rural communities it is impossible to cash a personal check drawn on a metropolitan bank without having either a local account or a local citizen to authorize the check. This fact comes as a shock to many "substantial" individuals who immediately make a bit of a scene and are carried away with their own importance. "Telephone my bank in the city, or my broker! He'll tell you my net worth." "Sorry, Charlie, it's bank policy. No account, you'll have to wait till the check clears for your money." The old refrain.

Simply open the account in the country bank and from that point on you will be treated as a member of the Rockefeller family. If you wish the red-carpet treatment, deposit a few extra thousand and you will receive a personal letter from the President—not of the United States, but of the bank.

It's quite likely that you have lived in the same apartment or co-op for the past fifteen years and haven't the slightest idea who lived across the hall or in the apartment above or below you. Now that you are in the country, introduce yourself and your family to your neighbors in the immediate vicinity of your property. It is not at all necessary that this neighborly gesture be accomplished with the aid of a three-piece band, an out-of-town caterer and a lawn cocktail party. Simply drive down the road, knock on the door, and pass the time of day. Advise your new friends and neighbors not to hesitate to call upon you in time of need.

Critical or derogatory remarks to local country people concerning the community, the people, the local government, taxes, roads, the climate or the number of mosquitoes should be kept at a minimum until your presence in the community has been well established. A rural community may be compared to the huge family, most of whom are not on speaking terms. The relatives have the privilege of calling their own family members every name in the book, but no outsider has the right to speak even one harsh word against any member of the clan.

If you plan to attend any local community meetings or airings in reference to ordinances, zoning or schools, good judgment dictates that you don't monopolize the time offered to the citizens to speak their opinions. Blend any critical remarks with a few well-chosen compliments. If you must be aggressive, do it tactfully and without dealing in personalities.

Refrain from writing public notices or letters to the editor of the local newspaper as a means to accomplish a local result. A personal conversation with your local government representative for your district or area will accomplish a great deal, and without antagonizing 50 percent or more of the community who might not share your opinion, for one reason or another.

Investigate thoroughly all invitations to be a member of a local planning, zoning or improvement committee. Local town boards use the committee method to get the irate citizenry off their backs and pass the buck to a powerless group. Don't let your ego become inflated when asked to join such a committee. It's quite likely that all those asked before you wouldn't touch it with a ten-foot pole!

It isn't necessary for you to erect a billboard type of sign that inscribes your family name or description of your country place in twelve-foot letters. Just simply put your name on the rural mailbox and the neighbors will be happy.

Almost all substantial country-property and landowners

have no objection to their neighbor's using open spaces and woods on their property for hiking, snowmobiling, fishing, horseback riding or bicycling. Fences in the country are usually to confine cattle, horses and other stock within the premises, *not* to keep the neighbors out. This custom should be enjoyed and mutually shared only if permission is given and a clear-cut understanding of use has been established, to avoid friction. I would discourage erecting permanent type fencing around the borders of your property if the sole purpose of the action taken is to establish property lines. Trees, shrubs or hedges will serve the same purpose and be much more in keeping with the country environment.

Utility companies will program a lighting system of high-intensity lights for you that will make your property resemble Yankee Stadium when completed, if you so desire. In addition to accommodating night football and baseball games, it will also attract every known insect within twenty miles to your front door, and buckshot from your neighbors.

Swimming pools, basketball courts, tennis courts, riding rings, dog kennels, dancing pavilions, musical and recording studios are but a few of the goodies that have followed the city dweller to the country. If they are part of your scene, or will be, plan their placement in such a way that they will have the least effect on the passing public and the neighbors.

If you have a driveway and parking area, use it. Don't permit vehicles to be parked along the public road. In addition to the danger involved to persons and property, you will be tagged a local nuisance.

You will frequently encounter every size, shape and

form of farm vehicle using the local town and country roads. The farmer is transporting his goods and wares from one location to another, or from one farm to another. His tractor and wagon on the road may not be entirely legal, but that is the way of the country. If you find in driving that you are following this obstacle on the highway, and there isn't room to pass, simply have patience. Don't land on your horn as you would at Madison Avenue and 49th Street. You will find he's only going a short distance and will be relieving your blood pressure at the nearest open field. *Please remember this.* Most people in the country pass the time of day with a friendly honk of the horn or a personal greeting, whether they know who you are or not. You will find this is a unique experience and will want to join the Friendly Sons of the Soil.

School buses are commonplace in the early hours of the morning and midafternoon on all country roads during the school year. Most state laws do not permit a driver to pass in either direction while the school bus is picking up or depositing pupils. Watch out for the children!

When employing local domestic and other help remember that the General-Private relationship is not in keeping with the country. Genuine kindness and attention should be shown. Country employees resent a haughty, cold, indifferent attitude. They react most favorably to being treated as a member of the family.

Be patient with servicemen and suppliers. They are usually not quite as punctual as you would like. An early morning cup of coffee or an afternoon cold drink will do wonders for your relationship with these people, and will be a blessing in times of emergency and need.

A good habit that is universally acceptable—pay all your

bills promptly. Avoid uncomfortable financial situations with local people by asking them, "How much?" in advance of ordering material or engaging services.

The genuine country resident abides by the adage, "A man's word is his bond." Keep yours. Keep all appointments on time and accept in full the responsibilities of your previous commitments. At all times be the perfect gentleman and lady in the company of local people. (Other times, have a ball, if you wish!)

Inactive or active membership in a local church or synagogue and one or two community services is recommended. This participation will be indicative of your interest in becoming an integral part of the community. Send a minimum donation to your local volunteer fire company and ambulance service. The people of the community give their time, skills and lives to these organizations that are usually supported only by contributions. Small donations to other worthwhile local functions are also recommended. The amount of the donation is not as important as contributing conservatively to many community activities.

Your lifetime longing for pets, horses or chickens may now be fulfilled with your purchase of a place in the country. Please keep them within the boundaries of your property and avoid lawsuits and unpleasantness as a result of their straying on the highway or on neighbors' properties, destroying their gardens, or nipping their children. Give serious thought before becoming involved with demonstrations in rural areas. Most country personalities have not succumbed to placard-carrying protesters. You will discover that country representatives do their best to satisfy their constituents in an orderly and procedural fashion. Politics may make strange bedfellows, but don't carry your couch on your back.

Local merchants have a country way of giving to you or your children small material tokens of appreciation. Accept them graciously, if offered, and don't insist on paying for the package of lollipops or can of tobacco for your husband. By the same token, gratuities should not be overdone on your part for small favors. You will find that a warm thank-you note or personal, firm handshake is most accepted and meaningful.

Don't hesitate to offer your aid and assistance without

reservation to your neighbor, or other country resident. The disabled car along the road, a ride into town, a phone call or visit at a time of family tragedy, a kind and sympathetic word at all times of trouble speaks of your genuine interest in the community. Try to avoid borrowing heavy tools and equipment frequently from neighbors and friends.

Entertaining in the country is usually informal and relaxed. Stay away from country bars and saloons. They are off limits to most newcomers. You will find plenty of attractive and appropriate local restaurants and cocktail lounges to accommodate your thirst for a tall glass of ice-cold buttermilk.

If you are planning to be away for any extended period of time during the growing season, make arrangements to have your lawns mowed. Country places look their best when tidy. Most neighbors want to be proud of their community's appearance.

Until you become acquainted personally with the people in the community, you will be referred to, probably, as "the people who bought the Jones place" or "the folks from the city." Introduce yourself and members of your family modestly, as opportunities present themselves. Before long it will seem you have lived in the country all your lives. Surprisingly, you will find yourself saying the same thing about the new people from the city who buy the "Smith place" down the road from you.

Last, but not least, whatever you do in the country, for heaven's sake—

Smile!

21

THE LITTLE THINGS

"Ah, sweet mystery of life, at last I've found you!" sings the male partner in the couple from the city. But before the duet is complete with full harmony, let's clear up a few doubts that might be in the back of the mind of wife and mother concerning her happiness in this strange, new country life.

Domestic help, baby-sitters, gardeners and handymen are available without too much difficulty in most country areas on an hourly, per diem or weekly basis. Country children spend most of their spare time working at home, or making themselves available to those seeking services. Their lives differ from their city cousins in the variety of chores and early responsibilities to which they are exposed. From early childhood they are reminded that a healthy, strong working body makes for a strong mind. They make wonderful mother's helpers.

To find assistance it is recommended that you put an

ad in the local newspaper, contact the nearest high school, employment office, Scout troop, or ask any local neighbor with a large family as to the availability of part-time help. Young college students from nearby institutions of learning are always eager to make extra money on weekends or during the summer.

The attitude and performance of country help is quite different from that which you can find in the cities. You will appreciate the warm, dedicated capability in both the young and adult job seekers.

As for medical services, the country-doctor image with his horse and buggy is still very much present and available, although the real man is far more mobile. You will want to introduce yourself to him on your arrival in the community. This acquaintance will give you peace of mind, knowing that the doctor will recognize you when you need him, that you won't be just a call from a stranger in the night. Country physicians *do* make house calls in emergencies and in some areas for routine procedures. Yes, shortages do exist in some areas, but our experience has been that medical comfort and care is there when you really need it. It is not our intention to paint a picture of impending appendectomies nor fractured collarbones, but it is good to know that most rural areas are served with excellent community hospitals and clinics with the added protection of highly trained, skilled volunteer ambulance services.

You will find an adequate supply of good country grocery stores and branches of major supermarkets in neighboring towns and villages. The local grocer or butcher is usually a jolly and folksy person who will be a most helpful friend. From springtime through autumn the roadside farm markets are a joy to the shopper, offering homegrown vegetables, fruits, flowers, plants and shrubs in colorful variety at a fraction of city costs.

Friends for your children naturally are on top of your list. An occasional weekend guest does not solve the problem of happy companionship for youngsters, to say nothing of what a steady stream of little friends from the city might do to your own peace, serenity and refrigerator. If you're starting out cold in the community, just ask your broker, attorney, doctor, insurance agent, grocer or neighbor to introduce you to families from the city with children in the same age bracket as your own. Not only will your children have others to play with, and places to go, but you and your husband will make interesting, stimulating new friends with parents quite possibly in the same boat. Recreational areas also offer an opportunity for your children to meet new friends and develop country relationships.

By all means subscribe to your local and county newspapers before and after making the move to the countryside. Mailed to your city address while you are in process of purchase, these papers are a great source of information in planning places to go, things to do, where to obtain services, besides local color and humor at its best.

There is a normal tendency to want to share with your many friends and relations in the city your newfound joy and happiness with your country home. But beware of the crowds. While your husband is telling everyone in the office, "I can't wait for you to see the place! Bring the wife and kids next weekend," you're probably extending the same invitation to the bridge club, to say nothing of your three sisters and their families. It invariably happens, after a half-dozen weekends of a steady stream of honking horns, "We're here!" and, "Don't fuss for lunch—we brought the charcoal for a barbecue," that you're ready for a nice quiet weekend alone at your home in the city.

A metropolitan physician recently told me that he had so many guests who introduced themselves as relatives, bombarding his country home, he was seriously thinking of giving them blood tests on arrival to determine their authenticity!

There is sometimes a bit of apprehension about women being alone in the country for any length of time. This fear is not well founded. The crime rate in most rural areas is practically nil. If they would make you more relaxed, buy a couple of barking dogs. They'll scare away prowlers and unwanted guests.

The instances of vandalism and burglary while your home is left uninhabited from time to time are relatively few. A few lamps left on and a neighbor's child checking the place during the week are the usual procedures to follow and all the insurance you'll need. If you are planning to be away for an extended period of time, contact your local state police, who do an admirable job of keeping your property under surveillance. Remember, the more isolated and remote your property, the greater the risk of possible forced entry.

For your personal needs, such as an occasional shampoo and set, there are many capable women who operate clean, licensed, up-to-date beauty parlors in their country homes. Just pick up your party-line telephone for information regarding the one nearest you.

Auctions, antique shows, flea markets, summer and winter stock, art classes, ski schools, riding academies,

golf and tennis are but a few of the activities available in the country to fill the "lonely moments" you might anticipate, if you have any!

You will enjoy attending the country church of your faith for a multitude of reasons. The simplicity of the architecture, the wholesomeness of the country parishioner, the down-to-earth priest or preacher will leave you completely refreshed after a Sunday morning service. Many community activities are centered around the local churches. You'll want to bring the whole family to enjoy such highlights as the Summer Strawberry Festival, Attic and Barn Rummage Sale, or Annual Picnic and Clambake.

Believe me, you haven't lived until you've attended the Friday Night Square Dance at the firehouse or town hall! So treat yourself to a swinging peasant dress for the new look and a good old-fashioned hoedown, or, better yet, wait to explore some of the interesting boutiques and smart dress shops contained in private homes in the country. You might even open one yourself!

22

CAN I MAKE A LIVING IN THE COUNTRY?

There are no shortcuts to success anywhere short of *damn hard work!*

This is my stock reply to civil engineers, brokers, advertising executives, computer programmers, corporate and business executives, and many others who believe they have reached the point of no return to their city positions and want to "pack it all in" for a new permanent way of life in the country. Some of their motivations are carbon copies of the front-page stories in their city newspapers, ranging from stalled commuter trains to wives and children being mugged on the streets and in the public schools.

Simply to escape the pressures, tensions and problems of the cities *does not* itself justify a radical transplant from one place to live and work to another, without giving due consideration to the necessary economic, social, cultural, educational and psychological adjustments. Making a living in the country is only one small piece of the total crossword puzzle of life. I suggest, therefore, that you well consider the following observations that I have made during the past many years by touching personally the best and worst of both city and country life, and sharing the experiences of those families who might have leaped too quickly.

Weigh each of the statements of fact and condition as they affect every member of your family. Remember, uprooting an entire way of life deserves microscopic self-screening if happiness and peace of mind are to be achieved along the way.

1. Salary scale for the employee and gross income for the entrepreneur are substantially less in rural areas than in major metropolitan communities. True, the cost of living is generally less in the country, but it doesn't entirely close the gap.

2. Opportunities for advancement in employment and rapid growth in business and profession are much greater in heavily populated areas.

3. Many diversified educational institutions in the cities provide the city inhabitant with the opportunity of study and instruction on a part-time basis while gainfully employed or self-employed. Country areas do not offer these bonuses.

4. In-city communities have colleges, universities and trade schools that one's children may attend on a full-time basis and still be able to live at home, thus relieving some of the enormous cost burdens of away-from-home college expenses

5. Cultural centers for music, art, drama, etc., offer the city family many opportunities to broaden their horizons. We are all becoming victims of convenience and will partake accordingly. The rural community cannot support many of the luxuries of the mind, and to find intellectual stimulation requires country peo-

ple to travel a good distance if they wish to satisfy their appetite for culture.

6. The opportunity to highly specialize in any one profession, business or occupation is limited in less populated areas because of lack of financing by sponsors, technical facilities in which to function, community attitude and appreciation, and insufficient demand for services.

7. The technical and specialized services rendered by many working wives and mothers in the cities command excellent pay and intellectual stimulation in opportunities and challenges. The small-town areas do not open these doors, simply because the need is not there.

8. The public-school system in the big cities today is faced with insurmountable problems. It is certainly impossible for even the well above average family to finance private-school education. The country public-school systems *are* experiencing some problems, but are maintaining a wholesome way of school life for the students. Private day-schools in most rural areas that are easily accessible are generally nonexistent. Those of you who are willing to make the financial sacrifice for what you believe will give your children the best education in private school will have to face the reality that this type of education is not readily available in country areas.

9. An active social life is an integral part of many city families' existence. Although people in the country do not lock themselves up in closets, consideration should be given that social life in the city and social life in the country are two different worlds.

10. Your day-to-day habits and customs of dress, shopping, recreation, religious affiliations, entertaining, obligations involving family and friends will be drastically changed by any major move from the city to the countryside. It may be the greatest thing that ever hap-

pened to your family, but much discussion and thought must be given prior to the great decision.

11. It is most unlikely that the breadwinner of the family will be able to find work in the country comparable to what he has known in his city position. I have witnessed many men whose desire to remove from the city (not from their job, occupation or profession) was so intense that they sacrificed substantial pension rights, advancement opportunities, stock options, life-insurance protection, major-medical insurance and many other benefits without serious consideration to the value to themselves or families. These snap decisions were made in many instances prior to investigation of what was ahead on the road to the countryside—which introduces Number 12.

12. A family must study, investigate and review a country community of their choice with as much thoroughness as a major corporation would in considering relocating a major plant. The advice of local bankers, accountants, attorneys, civic, business and professional leaders should be sought for the purpose of obtaining a warehouse of information relating to the community, specific employment, professional or business opportunities, future growth, known hazards, and the dozens of other facts that will have a direct bearing on your decision for your future life. Prior to any major decision, it is advisable that you rent a comfortable apartment or home with the idea of spending as much leisure time as possible in the community and observe as a resident, although part-time, the overall way of life. Make every effort to become friendly with as many people as possible. Their experiences, attitudes and knowledge will prove invaluable.

13. If you are desirous of purchasing an *existing venture,* retain the services of a well-established accounting firm and an attorney for a thorough review, analysis

and guidance. Discuss your interest with at least two local bankers and obtain from them opinions as to all phases of the enterprise. Starting a *new venture* in a community that is both strange and new to you should be done *only* after you have exhausted every possible source of information relating to its need and potential. Those seeking opportunities in retail businesses will find the going generally difficult, especially in areas where major shopping centers are springing up at a rapid rate. The rural population today is very mobile. People are no longer dependent upon the local small-town store owner who cannot compete in selection or price with the chain stores.

14. Specific job, professional or business opportunities (and Heaven knows there are hundreds!) must be reviewed and investigated. Federal, state and local employment offices, civil-service divisions, professional and trade journals, newspapers are but a few major sources of opportunity information.

15. Before you lock the door behind you and throw away the key, be sure of what lies ahead.

I firmly believe that if anyone (regardless of trade or calling) wants to earn a living in the country, it can be done. But whether the individual and/or his family wants to make certain sacrifices is another story. Happiness anywhere can only be found and defined within the individual. The purpose of this chapter was to serve as a caution light for those of you who might be inclined to leap before you look and for others who believe naïvely that happiness is a permanent place in the country.

23

THE COUNTRY AND
THE GOLDEN YEARS

Our statisticians are telling us that people are living longer and retiring earlier. The big question to be answered by our senior citizens and their children is *where to spend the golden years?* Many couples are today buying country property in anticipation of retirement. They are making this decision well in advance of permanent occupancy, using the facility in the interim for weekends and vacations. An early move in this direction has proven to be a wise one, considering inflation and spiraling costs of construction.

Many factors over the past twenty years have influenced retired people to leave cities where they have spent all of their lives, to take up residence far removed from their lifelong neighborhoods and customs. These people find the cities difficult to endure at a time when peace and quiet are sought most. The high cost of apartment and home living in the major cities is an extreme hardship for retired people with a fixed income.

Mother and Dad are daily warned by their children not to go out for an evening walk for fear of being mugged. The afternoon in the park is no longer a pleasant experience, with purse snatchers and hoodlums in the background. It is no longer practical for them to own an automobile while living in some of the major cities. The high cost of insurance and parking, coupled with traffic congestion, discounts the advantages of automobile ownership in town.

What does the country have to offer the retirement couple, widow, or widower? There are thousands of wonderful small towns and villages in country areas throughout our great United States that offer a wide range of living accommodations. The majority of the younger set emphasize acreage and privacy surrounding their country homes. Therefore, the demand for the one- or two-family homes in the villages, with a large backyard and quiet setting, has been steadily decreasing. The village property, therefore, by the law of supply and demand, has not been subject to a radical increase in price. Properties of this type have remained stable or even lowered in price over the past five years.

The country village should be seriously considered for a retirement home or apartment for many reasons:

1. Housing accommodations are usually within walking distance of stores and banks.
2. There is neighborly companionship that is friendly, warm and helpful.
3. The local doctor, dentist, post office, pharmacy, church and other frequently needed services are usually within an arm's length.

4. Domestic help, practical nurses and handymen are usually available and most accommodating.
5. Full- or part-time employment for those seeking meaningful activity is usually available at the local lumber yard, liquor store, grocery market, dress shop, library or nearby farms.
6. The ownership of an automobile will give hours of pleasure along quiet country roads.
7. Garden parties, movies, church functions, firehouse activities, arts and crafts clubs, picnics, adult-education programs, volunteer hospital auxiliary service, local Red Cross, Cancer, Heart, TB and other community programs provide both volunteer and paid opportunities for service.

Those of you who are taking off to your country retreats every weekend and holidays, leaving retired parents back in the cities, might consider having them purchase or rent a comfortable country village home or apartment nearby. Your children will have more time to spend with their grandparents. You'll have a pair of built-in, adoring baby-sitters for special occasions. Nobody will feel neglected, and the total net advantage to the family will be tremendous.

In many larger rural communities there are retirement accommodations in lovely old homes that have been converted into residences for "refined ladies, and country-squire gentlemen." These are not nursing homes but residences for healthy, elderly people run by compassionate, capable owners of the property. Picture, if you will, a stately, tree-shaded, Victorian former mansion where a dozen or so active senior citizens have their own private accommodations, large recreational facilities, beautiful gardens, trees and lawns—and companionship! The owner serves family home-style meals to the guests and provides other personal services. The occupants have much in common and really have a great time planning their days' activities. These accommodations are *not* expensive, considering all the tangible and intangible benefits they offer.

If you're not the communal type, then consider a small country cottage that requires only a minimum of maintenance and care. A retirement couple might want to spend only six months of the year in the country and the rest of the time traveling or in some other locale. Many states have passed or are in process of adopting legislation granting local tax authorities the power to give substantial real estate tax concessions to those people owning their own homes who are retired, or sixty-five years of age or more. Investigate this opportunity to own your own home with very little or no real estate taxes!

There is also the possibility of renting out your cottage for that portion of the year you are not in occupancy, thus providing sufficient income to meet many of the operating expenses of your part-time home.

Loneliness is one of the major fears accompanying the "Golden Years." The conditions in the cities limit freedom of movement of retired persons. You will discover that the average country village and the people who live there will not permit you to have a lonely moment, if you give them half a chance.

A word of caution! Don't wait until the day after the testimonial retirement dinner to investigate and review what the country village has to offer. Start right now.

24

THE VACATION OR RETIREMENT HOME IN DEVELOPMENT COMMUNITIES

- Escape to country magnificence.
- Breathtaking four-season beauty.
- The perfect place for privacy, fun and relaxation.
- A world of rolling hills and cooling forests.
- Lake front, lake view or heavily wooded.
- A world of sea and sand.
- Back to nature.
- Where the good life begins.
- The sound of nature all around you.
- For the love of living.

Millions of Americans are responding to the call of the country to establish their vacation or retirement home. They are contributing to the "second-home" phenomenon with the same eager enthusiasm experienced when the "second-car" way of life started several years ago.

Massive vacation and retirement-home projects, offering snowmobiling, skiing, hiking, swimming and boating, are touching every level of our society—a luxury reserved for only the very rich not too long ago.

There are many sophisticated major developers dealing with thousands of acres of land with lakes, swimming pools, golf courses and other attractions that offer the development type community or cluster vacation or retirement facility. There are, however, the "shoestring" and "fly-by-night" complexes that are poorly planned, underfinanced and fraught with problems and complications that in your wildest imagination you could not believe existed.

I am particularly concerned with those of you who might be attracted, in all innocence, to buy a lot or home or build in the marginal development type project. Attorney Generals' offices throughout the country are being deluged with letters of complaint from irate purchasers with tales of woe and grief: homes that have been fully paid for but never finished; roads never completed; swimming pools promised but existing only in the brochure; lakes without water, even homes without water; raw sewage in open ditches; no utilities (electric and telephone); faulty deeds and conveyances; rodent and insect problems; basements filled with water; and mud instead of lawns.

How does our affluent society become a party to this type of involvement? Where are the laws to protect the naïve and innocent purchaser? How is it possible that a retired couple can be fleeced so easily of their life's savings? It is not my mission to answer these questions or philosophize as to the frailties of human nature. The procedure for you to follow to avoid being caught or hung is the primary purpose of this chapter.

Many undercapitalized and inexperienced development

ventures are initiated with the most honorable intentions. For hundreds of reasons too involved to specify the whole program falls apart. The project begins with engineers, architects, artists and a few model homes that *are* built to perfection. Decor and layouts cater to the taste of the most discriminating. The naïve purchasers are led to yet-to-be-developed Lot Number 17A. It is here the model home with desired changes will be erected within three months after they sign the contract and their lives away. All the other fringe benefits of the proposed development that surround the community will also be promised to be completed within a reasonable period of time.

If you are attracted to the general location, impressed by what you anticipate will be the end result of the development community, *before you move a step further* obtain the following information:

1. All aspects of the financial terms, such as down payment, mortgage provisions, interest rates, closing date, closing costs of "extras," special fees and name of financing institution or company.
2. Type of homes to be erected within the development and restrictions of property use for others becoming part of the project.
3. Roads to be constructed and who will be permanently responsible for maintaining them.
4. Complete plans and detailed specifications of home to be erected and construction procedures to be followed.
5. The names of principals involved in both the construction and the overall development.
6. Credit references—banks, suppliers and government agencies, etc.
7. Proof of approval of the project from health and other regulatory agencies.

8. Provisions for water supply and sewage disposal.
9. Names of bonding and insurance companies involved with performance, procedures and guarantees.
10. Copies of all maps, surveys and related information of your specific lot and the entire development.
11. Provisions to be made for fire and police protection, medical facilities, schools, shopping, public transportation, and other needed services.
12. Name of counsel representing the developers and builders.

The most serious problems associated with the second home or retirement community are those of waste disposal and good water. These problems have grown so bad in many communities throughout the United States in the past few years that entire areas had to be closed because of pollution. Very strict conservation and environmental control laws adopted by many states are serving to limit and curtail potential and in-being complications. Control of roads, water and waste disposal should be vested with public authorities or local governmental agencies. This method guarantees to the community continuity of quality and service for the minimum amount of expense to the resident. Private management of these items may be subject to unreasonable fees and irresponsible performance. Local governments usually outline their requirements with reference to water, sewage disposal and roads that must be met by the developers before they will assume ownership, control and responsibility for these three major necessities of any development.

Those developers who do not meet the required specifications are precisely the ones causing the big problems. The naïve purchaser is then right in the middle of what is being experienced in many areas today. For reasons of

but not limited to lack of funds, poor planning, management problems, many projects are stalled and only partially completed. This leaves the innocent bystander with little recourse but to write to legal authorities of his disappointments, frustrations and financial loss.

In their effort to provide an economic stimulant to the community, many local banking institutions have joined the red-faced citizens when a project falls flat on its face or goes bankrupt. Bank commitments are going to be based upon accomplishments and not upon projections after experience with those developers who do not have a long record of financial stability and success.

Local city fathers of rural communities are developing a more tongue-in-cheek attitude toward many of the glamorous wheeling-and-dealing promoters pouncing on a community with highly exaggerated and overzealous plans for a new community development. Past bitter experience that has come to light from other areas, or possibly their own, has prompted this wait-and-see conservative approach.

Try to avoid being a Daniel Boone participant in any new development—the risks are many. The attraction to the new project is usually a favorable offering price and many extras. It is part of the promotional scheme to get the project off the ground. Many recreational or retirement communities offer the use of lakes, skiing facilities, golf courses, beaches, health clubs, country clubs, stables, fishing and game preserves. Make certain what the cost of using these facilities will be and whether you are saddled with a pro rata charge for them whether you use them or not! Also, an idea what future costs might be.

Don't sign anything, regardless of how simple the docu-

**ments may appear, without the advice of counsel and a
bank officer in the community!**

The reliability of the developer and builder involved
in the project is the key to your retirement or vacation
home. Don't be afraid to ask those who have purchased
or built in the development what their reactions and experiences have been. Getting it from the horse's mouth is
invaluable.

Place particular attention on the restrictive provisions
accompanying your proposed deed. Limitations may be
involved with reference to the size and type of the structure to be built. It may require that you must build something substantially larger than you wish or can afford.
Are you allowed to rent your property? You may wish to
consider this possibility for part of the year for the purpose of deriving tax benefits and income. A facility used
solely for personal use is not subject to depreciation and
other tax-deductible allowances, but these benefits are
available pro rata if the house is rented for all or part of
the taxable year. Inquire as to whether this possibility
exists in accordance with the development restrictions and
the potential of such a plan, if desired.

In summary, **be careful, be cautious, be guided by the
best legal and banking opinion obtainable before buying!**

25

WHAT TO DO ABOUT CONDEMNATION AND EASEMENTS TO PUBLIC UTILITIES

Most federal and state government agencies, political subdivisions and public utilities have the legal right to take all or part of your property for public use—a power known as "eminent domain." You poor souls! You haven't had time yet to hang the pictures and I'm telling you you have to move. Sad, but true: your place in the sun could be in the way of the dozens of reasons for which property can be condemned. A few examples are new highways and roads, airports, public utilities' lines and services, hospitals, public housing projects, public parks and recreational areas, military establishments, and communication centers. It is not very likely you will be faced with this agonizing problem in the country, but it's always a possibility.

You should be well informed of the procedures to be followed in the event that the wheels of progress are turning into your front door. There is very little that you can do to stop a government agency or public utility from taking your property. But you can insist you be compensated at the market value of your property at the time of the take-over. The law provides that you must be paid a just and fair amount for the property involved. The computation of this amount is a variable that depends upon the agency involved and the laws governing that particular agency. The amount to be received by a property owner may be estimated by the following customary methods:

1. *Market value*—What a willing buyer would pay a willing seller under normal negotiating circumstances.
2. *Highest and best use*—Value of the property assuming its maximum future potential, if such potential can be reasonably projected.
3. *Relocation expenses*—Costs involved to the property owner in relocating home or business.
4. *Severance damages*—Awards where only a portion of total property is taken, an additional sum paid for any or all damages to remaining property.

The total compensation received under condemnation procedures may be one of the above methods or a combination of all of them, depending on the circumstances of the taking.

Who determines market value? The government agency or public utility will employ a team of expert appraisers who base their conclusions on the many court-accepted principles of appraising property.

You may, should, and have every right to agree or disagree with the government agency appraiser upon whose opinion the agency will base its preliminary offer for your property. If you agree to accept the offer, no problem. The transaction is handled in a routine manner. If, however, you, the property owner, disagree, your only line of action is to retain the services of a competent attorney highly skilled in condemnation procedures. The first step the attorney will probably take is to retain an independent firm of qualified appraisers. Their conclusions must be based on generally approved appraising standards acceptable in the courts. These matters have become very technical, and the property owner's opinion, or the opinion of even someone active in real estate transactions, but not highly qualified as an appraiser, are of no consequence in the courts where these matters will be decided.

The attorney representing the property owner will then determine, on the basis of facts supplied by the appraiser, whether to take formal legal court action or not. His appraiser's opinion might coincide with, or not differ substantially from, the offer made by the government agency or public utility. Since initiating or executing a court action in a condemnation procedure is a very costly business, the property owner might wind up with an amount equal to, or less than, the original government offer, after all costs and expenses of the action are paid, even though his own appraisal was higher than that of the government agency.

A competent attorney might settle or compromise prior to formal action in the courts. A government agency must recognize costs of court action and weigh all other possibilities before turning its back on a reasonable settlement.

I have heard many attorneys use these words of wisdom: "A good settlement is better than the best lawsuit." Rely upon the advice of counsel.

The opportunity for one to "reap a rich harvest" from

any government or utility agency is quite remote. In fact, one should consider oneself fortunate to receive what might be considered a good price for the property. There are many known inequities in the taking of property under "eminent domain" or other legal procedures, although many states, recognizing these inequities, are updating the procedures involved.

There are so many intangibles for which the unwilling seller is not compensated under existing laws. Think of the hundreds of irreplaceable treasures, ranging from the rock garden to the half-mile-long stone-wall fence that took years to build with loving toil and great personal satisfaction. The charm of a pre-Revolutionary home that cannot be duplicated or replaced. The two-centuries-old trees along the garden path that have been valued at two hundred dollars each by the government appraiser whose interest in trees is limited to Page 7 of his appraisal manual.

It must be very apparent to you at this point in the chapter where my sentiments lie in the complexity of condemnation. Better get back to the facts before three hundred pages are devoted to the taking of property.

In the event that part or all of your property is being considered for government or utility use, I would suggest the following dos and don'ts:

1. Do not become involved in any direct negotiations with any representative as to your intentions, values, purchase price requested or amount for which you will sell.
2. Do not sign any document without obtaining the advice of competent counsel.
3. Obtain as much information from the government or utility representative as possible without revealing anything to them but "name, rank and serial number."

4. If neighboring property owners are involved in the project, it is worthwhile to consider retaining one attorney under joint representation. Remember, in numbers there is strength.

5. Don't panic! The government moves very slowly and it might be only a preliminary survey, one of several sites under consideration.

6. Investigate thoroughly all costs involved before retaining counsel, experts or other outside advice.

The general opinion of all property owners affected by any major community move has more bearing today than it had ten or fifteen years ago because government leaders today are more sensitive to public opinion. Those who although not directly affected by a proposed improvement are concerned with the effect the proposed project might have on the ecology of their neighborhood may be most helpful in supporting your negative position. In any event, seek out the best available advice before making any snap decisions.

There is a strong possibility that the further expansion

of public utilities within rural areas will affect you in the immediate future. The country property owner is frequently approached by representatives from the power company, telephone service and gas companies. The usual request is for permission to install over, on, or through your property various poles, lines, wires or cables. The right to do so must be given by the property owner in writing and this right is known as an "easement" or "right-of-way." Once it is granted it is rather impossible to have revoked. The presence of this installation is usually unsightly or a nuisance.

Most public utilities are private corporations regulated by various federal or state agencies. **You do not have to give these utility companies the right to use your property without being justly compensated.** Do not grant any right or sign any papers without advice of counsel.

For many years people in the country, by custom, have given easements to public utilities for a total consideration of one dollar. Power poles have been strung from one end of their property to the other and have become permanent easements that are attached to and "run with" the transfer of the property.

Permitting underground cables on your property might someday interfere with a building project, swimming pool, water line, etc. Any easements granted public-utility companies by a prior owner should be investigated thoroughly by you and your attorney to determine their extent and nature.

In conclusion, if you relinquish any rights to your property, or interest therein, you must be fairly compensated accordingly. Discuss with your attorney any action that involves your rights before giving them up.

26

GLOSSARY

Abandoned Farm—Classification commonly given to parcel of real estate once occupied and used as a working farm that is now dormant, neglected, with buildings in poor state of repair. Might be indicative of being in process of foreclosure or under litigation.

Abstract of Title—A summary of the most important parts of all recorded instruments that affect the title to property, arranged in the order in which they were recorded.

Acre—A measure of land equal to 160 square rods, or 4,840 square yards, or 43,560 square feet. (A plot of land approximately 200 feet wide and 200 feet deep is nearly an acre.)

Adverse Possession—A means of acquiring title where an occupant has been in actual, open, notorious, exclusive and continuous occupancy of property under a claim of right for the required statutory period.

Agreement of Sale—A written agreement between seller and buyer in which the purchaser agrees to buy certain real estate, and the seller agrees to sell, upon terms and conditions set forth therein.

Amortization—A gradual paying off of a debt by periodic installments.

Apportionment—Adjustment of the income, expense or carrying charges of real estate, usually computed to the date of closing of title, so that the seller pays all expenses to that date. The buyer assumes all expenses commencing the date the deed is conveyed to him.

Appraisal—An estimate of a property's evaluation by an appraiser who is usually presumed to be expert in this work.

Appreciation—A rise in value or price attributable to such factors as inflation, market conditions, improvements, location, etc.

Assessor—An official who has responsibility of determining assessed values for purposes of taxation, etc.

Assumption of Mortgage—The taking of title to property by a grantee, wherein he assumes liability for payment of an existing note or bond, secured by a mortgage against a property, and becomes personally liable for the payment of such mortgage debt.

Barn Siding—Salvaged boards used in construction of old barns reconditioned or refinished for the purpose of making kitchen cabinets, doors, etc. in homes.

Bill of Sale—A written instrument given to pass title of personal property from seller to buyer.

Binder—An agreement to cover the payment of purchase of real estate as evidence of good faith on the part of the purchaser.

Blanket Mortgage—A single mortgage which covers more than one piece of real estate.

Bond—The evidence of a personal debt which is secured by a mortgage or other lien on real estate.

Boundary Line—The edge, border or limit of the property which may or may not be marked by fence, wall, road or trees.

Building Codes—Regulations established by local governments stating fully the strict requirements for building.

Building Line—A line fixed at a certain distance from the front and/or side of a lot beyond which no building can project.

Central School District—Apportioning of several towns, villages or areas into one major school facility under the jurisdiction of one school board and taxing authority. This system has replaced the operation of many small country schools with students now being bused to a central school facility.

Certiorari Proceedings—A proceeding to review in a competent court the action of an inferior tribunal board or officer exercising judicial functions, widely used by property owners contesting real estate assessments on their property made by local assessors.

Cesspool—A deep hole in the ground to receive drainage or sewage from the sinks, toilets, etc. of a house, normally found many years ago where public sewerage systems or septic tanks were not available. Use of cesspools today not permitted by law in many areas.

Chain of Title—A history of conveyances and encumbrances affecting a title from the time the original title was granted, or as far back as records are available.

Chattel Mortgage—A mortgage on personal property.

Circa—Term used to indicate an approximate date of construction of home or buildings. (Circa 1850).

Cistern—A large receptacle to serve as a reservoir for water. Source usually rain water collected from gutters on buildings. Main source of water many years ago prior to public water systems or wells.

Closing Date—The date upon which the buyer takes over the property, usually about thirty to sixty days after the signing of the contract.

Cloud on Title—An outstanding claim or encumbrance which, if valid, would affect or impair the owner's title.

Commitment—A pledge, or a promise, or an affirmation agreement.

Condemnation—Taking private property for public use with fair compensation to the owner. The exercised right of "eminent domain."

Contract—An agreement between competent parties to do or not to do certain things for a legal consideration, whereby one party acquires a right to what the other possesses.

Conveyance—The transfer of title of land from one to another. The means or medium by which title of real estate is transferred.

Covenants—Agreements written into deeds and other instruments promising performances, or nonperformances, of certain acts, or stipulating certain uses or nonuses of the property.

Credit Check—Procedure taken by lending institutions in mortgage applications and other requests for financing whereby the personal and financial history of an applicant is obtained and evaluated to determine credibility and risk factors based upon past credit experience.

Deed—An instrument in writing duly executed and delivered that conveys title to real property.

Deed Restriction—An imposed restriction in a deed for the purpose of limiting the use of the land. For example, a restriction as to the size, type, value or placement of improvements that may be erected thereon.

Deer Run—Established path, road or trail frequently used by deer in their search for water, food, etc.

Depreciation—Loss in value of real property brought about by age, physical deterioration, or financial or economic obsolescense.

Directional Growth—The location or direction toward which the residential sections of an area are destined or determined to grow.

Dirt Road—Private or public road in use in many rural areas that has not been surfaced with tar, concrete, asphalt and the like. Oil is being widely used on dirt roads to keep dust at a minimum during dry-season periods.

Dry Well—A hole in the ground filled with rocks or stones into which surface water or water from drainpipes on buildings is directed away from home or buildings to relieve potential water seepage into cellars. Water in dry wells eventually dissipates into the soil.

Earnest Money—Down payment made by a purchaser of real estate as evidence of good faith.

Easement—A right that may be exercised by the public or individuals on, over or through the lands of others. (Most common example, power or utility lines.)

Electrical Service—Source of electric power furnished by public or private utility company to property owner.

Eminent Domain—Right of the government to acquire property for necessary public use by condemnation. The owner must be fairly compensated.

Encroachment—A building, part of a building, or obstruction which intrudes upon or invades property of another.

Encumbrance—Any right to or interest in land that diminishes its value.

Equity—The interest or value which the owner has in real estate over and above the liens against it.

Erosion—The wearing away of land through the process of nature as by streams and winds.

Escrow—A written agreement between two or more parties providing that certain instruments or properties be placed with a third party to be delivered to a designated person upon the fulfillment or performance of some act or condition.

Escrow Account—A special financial account maintained by a lending institution, funded usually from a portion of the monthly mortgage payment of the borrower. The institution pays from this fund on behalf of the borrower obligations of taxes, insurance, etc., as they become due.

Firewood—Logs that are obtained from trees that are commonly used in wood-burning stoves or fireplaces. Not all standing trees are suitable for this purpose.

Gravity Flow—Usually associated with flow of water from a source such as a spring or well located at a higher elevation than the home or buildings into which the water supply flows by pipe or ditch.

Grazing Rights—The legal privilege or right granted one that permits the feeding of one's animals on the lands owned by another. Could be considered an encumbrance depending upon extent of legal circumstances.

Grievance Day—Period of time usually limited to one to three days designated by local taxing authorities to give property owners an opportunity to formally protest tax assessments. Notice of "grievance day" is usually well publicized in advance. Property owners may contact office of taxing authority to obtain "grievance day" dates if normal source of publications not available or subscribed to.

Growing Period or Season—The time, usually designated in number of months, during which agricultural crops, plants, vegetables, etc., may be planted and mature. Growing season directly related to the climate of any specific area and of particular interest to those directing their attention to the use of the soil.

Handyman Special—A frequently used description by those engaged in the sale of real estate, indicating to potential buyers a type of property that might appeal to those capable of performing themselves much-needed work to structure or structures. It is further indicative of an attractive purchase price "as is." Inquiry should be made in advance of inspection as to total general condition.

Hard Water—Condition of water usually found in many areas obtained from drilled wells that is *not* conducive for producing soap suds for washing clothes, dishes and bathing, although might be perfectly acceptable for human consumption. Note: see **water softener** below.

High-Tension Wires—Cable-like wires used for the transmission of inter- or intrastate high-voltage electric power; normally strung on enormous towers erected on property acquired by purchase, lease or easement. Utility companies claim there is no particular danger involved in their being near occupied private property, but generally they are a deterrent to property appeal when in obvious existence.

Interest Rate—The percentage of a sum of money charged for its use.

Lake Frontage—The legal ownership or right (usually measured in feet) which the property owner has in the real estate bordering the edge of a lake.

Lake Rights—The legal privilege or right granted to one who may or may not be a property owner on or near a lake to use the facility for swimming, fishing, boating, etc.

Leach Field—The area of ground or soil associated with a septic-tank system through which water and other liquids flow from the septic tank and dissipate into the soil. If the nature of the soil is not conducive to rapid dispatch of liquids—such as heavy clay, rock or shale—a series of ditches must be dug and filled with sand and stone to create the proper environment for a good functioning disposal system.

Lightning Rods—A sophisticated system installed on homes or buildings in many rural areas for protection against being struck by lightning. Usually installed by professionals specializing in this service. A number of metal rods are installed on the roofs of buildings and "grounded" to divert bolts of lightning from striking the roof's surface. Many fire-insurance companies will grant low premium rates if rods are installed properly. Note: Strongly recommended, but obtain service estimates.

Manicured Estate—An advertising cliché implying that the real estate offered for sale is in excellent state of repair, exceptionally attractive, well landscaped, expensive and substantial in nature.

Marketable Title—A title which a court of equity considers to be so free from defect that it will ensure its acceptance by a purchaser.

Metes and Bounds—A term used in describing the boundary lines of land, setting forth what the boundary lines are, together with their terminal points and angles.

Mildew—A thin, furry, whitish coating or discoloration appearing on organic matter especially when exposed to extreme dampness. A condition that should give serious concern to potential buyers of country homes if observed or detected when they are inspecting property. Indicates a possible water-seepage condition or other problem that might or might not be easily remedied.

Milky Water—A milky quality or state of main source of water attributable to various underground mineral conditions such as heavy limestone deposits, etc. *Does not* indicate impurity or unfitness for human consumption. May be observed simply by allowing water from faucets to run freely for several minutes before filling normal glass for inspection.

Mineral Rights—A legal privilege granted to one to remove, mine, or explore various subterranean minerals or like deposits. Holder of such rights may or may not have title to the property involved. A purchaser of property could possibly be subject to giving up his rights to another for the purpose of extracting from the earth certain minerals if the legal status as explained above exists.

Modular Unit or Construction—Factory-manufactured and factory-assembled section or sections of a housing unit built off-site; extensively used today for rapid construction of homes, apartment houses, office buildings, etc. Widely accepted and approved by contractors, building industry and government financing agencies. Note: Like everything else—as good as the reliability of manufacturer and installer. Investigate thoroughly before accepting.

Monument—A fixed object and point established by surveyors to establish land location.

Mortgage—An instrument in writing, duly executed and delivered, that guarantees a lien upon real estate as security for the payment of a specified debt. It is usually in the form of a bond.

Mortgage Commitment—A formal indication by a lending institution that it will grant a mortgage loan on property in a certain specified amount and on certain specified terms.

Mortgagee—A party who lends money and takes a mortgage to secure the payment thereof.

Mortgagor—A person who borrows money and gives a mortgage on his property as security for the payment of the debt.

Multiple Listing—An arrangement among a group of real estate brokers whereby each broker presents his listing of property for sale to the attention of the others with a prearranged agreement pertaining to the sharing of commissions. If properly administered this system affords purchaser in dealing with one broker the exposure of all property available within a certain area. The effectiveness of this program ranges from very poor to excellent, depending upon the brokers involved.

Option—A right given or a consideration to purchase or lease a property upon specified terms within a specified time. If the right is not exercised, the option holder is not subject to liability for damages. If exercised, the grantor of option must perform.

Party Line—The type of public telephone service available in many rural areas that lack extensive equipment and lines to provide for individual private service. The party-line customer *must* share the use of telephone service with several other customers on the same "line." On a party line, each customer has a separate and distinct number, but only one on the same line may receive or make an outgoing call in the event that no other customer on that line is using the service. Each customer is given a number of rings designation to identify the recipient of an incoming call.

Personal Property—Any property which is not real property.

Pond—An enclosed body of water smaller than a lake, often artificially formed.

Pond Site—An area conducive to the construction of a pond. Determination of pond site may be intelligently made only by experts in soil testing, engineering, surveying and the like. Suggested potential pond sites are often given without investigation of feasibility.

Posted Land—All or part of public or private lands that *do not* permit trespassing for the purpose of hunting, fishing, camping or other similar activities. Notice to the public is given by tacking "posted" signs or placards at regular intervals on trees or fences along the boundary of the property.

Prepayment Clause—A clause in a mortgage which gives a mortgagor the privilege of paying the mortgage indebtedness before it becomes due.

Private Road—A road or path used for egress and ingress that is owned and maintained by private owners. Persons other than owners could be construed as trespassers. Responsibility of snow removal and general maintenance rests with the owner at his own cost and expense.

Property Taxes—Taxes levied and collected from owners of real property administered by one or a combination of taxing authorities. Amounts and methods of taxation vary from one particular locale to another.

Public Road—A road owned and maintained by a governmental authority over which the public has unrestricted use, providing limitations such as weight, type of vehicle, etc. have not been placed. Responsibility for maintenance, snow removal, paving, drainage, etc., rests with public authority.

Purchase Money Mortgage—A mortgage given by someone purchasing real property in part payment of the purchase price of real estate.

Real Property—Land and generally whatever is erected upon or affixed thereto.

Recording—The act of writing or entering in a book of public record instruments affecting the title to real property.

Recording Fees—Costs involved in the recording of various legal documents such as mortgages, deeds, leases, options, etc., in the public-records office of a community.

Release Clause—A clause found in a blanket mortgage which gives the owner of the property the privilege of paying off a portion of the mortgage indebtedness and thus freeing a portion of the property from the mortgage.

Rescue Squad—A usually well-trained group of volunteer citizens of a community who accept the responsibility of providing free ambulance and other emergency services. Perform exemplary services to most rural communities throughout the United States. They may have available to them ultramodern equipment and facilities financed by public donation. Recognized and praised nationally by service organizations, government authorities and members of the medical profession. Volunteer rescue squads are the pride of every community in which they function.

RFD—Rural Free Delivery—an address designation in many rural areas used by postal authorities in the process of delivering mail to country individual locations. Sections of a postal area within a community might be called RFD 1, 2, 3, etc.

Riding Trails—Paths or roads created by extensive travel, or construction, or land clearance, used for the purpose of horseback riding, snowmobiling, skiing, etc. It is usually implied that these trails are within the confines of one's private property.

Right-of-way—The right to pass over another's land, more or less freely, according to the nature of the easement.

Riparian owner—One who owns land bounding upon a river or watercourse.

Road Frontage—The distance usually measured in feet

or miles that a parcel of private property adjoins a public or private road. It *should not* be assumed that the private lands, although adjoining, have accessibility by normal means to the public or private road. Deep ravines or gullies, sharp inclines or mountains might make accessibility impossible or difficult. Substantial road frontage *usually* greatly enhances the market value of the property, providing that the topography of the roads into the private lands blend well to complement the use of each. Good road frontage on *both sides* of public or private roads further increases the value of the property as this affords privacy and protection.

Road Grade—Private property is often referred to as being *above* or *below* road grade. Above road grade means that the private lands adjoining the road have a higher elevation than the normal grade of the road. Below grade means that the area of private ownership adjoining the road is below the level of the normal road grade in existence. There are both advantages and disadvantages to each elevation in accessibility, construction problems, drainage, noise, dirt and accident hazards.

Rolling Terrain—A frequently used description of land in real estate advertisements and brochures. The reader has a right to assume that the property being described has a combination of level, hilly, low and mini-mountain land. A further assumption can be reasonably made that one does not have to be a mountain climber or deep-sea diver to walk the property.

School Taxes—Taxes levied against property owners that are used to support the operation of the school district in which the property is located. Method of assessment and collection varies from one taxing authority district to another.

Screening—Term frequently used by country property

owners meaning the planting of rapid-growing trees, hedges or bushes that will serve to block out disturbing, unsightly or undesirable views, buildings or activities from key vantage points of the property.

Septic Tank—A tank in which waste matter is putrified and decomposed through bacterial action. Most common method of individual sewage-disposal system employed where public sewerage facilities are not available. Tank is buried in the ground within a short distance from the house and varies in size from five hundred to one thousand gallons' capacity. Water and other liquids flow from tank into below-surface area known as leach field and are dissipated into the ground.

Septic-Tank Cleanout—Access cap to septic tank—it may or may not be visibly exposed—by which professional septic-tank cleaners gain access for periodic maintenance and cleaning. New purchaser of property should obtain from former owner location of same prior to final acquisition of property.

Service Buildings—Descriptive term commonly used in advertising rural property, meaning sheds, barns, stables, garages, etc., in addition to main residence.

Setback—The distance from the property border, curb, road or other established line within which no buildings may be erected in accordance with deed restrictions, building codes, local ordinances or other various regulations. Purpose of a setback restriction is to avoid structures or homes being built too close to one another, to protect access views and to protect owner in the event of widening of roads by public authorities.

Stagnant Water—Water that becomes foul from lack of motion or current. Improperly constructed ponds, existing swamps and low areas produce stagnant water that is most undesirable. These areas are breeding grounds for rodents, insects and odors and should be disposed of or corrected as quickly as possible.

Star Route—A postal designation used for mail-delivery purposes for those residing along certain public highways.

Stocked Pond—A pond in which one or more varieties of fish have been placed by property owner. Usually indicates that the pond is not stagnant and is served by a plentiful supply of water from stream or springs. Many state and local fish and game departments make available supplies of fish and information relating to their care and the species appropriate for the area and environment.

Stone Wall—A formation of rocks, stones and slabs varying in length, width and height found on many rural properties; it was hand-built many years ago and served at that time as a "boundary line marker" or fence. Usually constructed without the use of masonry, the weight of each stone supporting the structure. Generally attractive and picturesque; stones from them have been used extensively the past few years for construction of fireplaces, patios, barbecue pits, chimneys and facings for homes and buildings.

Subdivision—A tract of land divided into lots or plots, suitable for home-building purposes.

Submersible Pump—A pumping apparatus usually operated electrically that is installed in the depth of a well for the purpose of pumping water from its level in the ground through plastic or metal pipes into home or buildings.

Sulfur Water—The designation given the type of water, obtained from drilling a well, that produces an undesirable sulfur-like smell and taste. This usually has no direct relationship with its bacterial fitness for human consumption. A condition that may be peculiar to certain areas in various states, but difficult to determine its existence prior to drilling an individual well. Several corrective filter systems are available to remove odor and taste, with results varying in relationship to severity of the condition.

Sump Pump—A pumping apparatus installed in a rather shallow hole or trench below the surface of a cellar floor in homes. Used with much success where surface or other water has a tendency to seep naturally under or through building foundations. Pump automatically starts when incoming water reaches a certain height in hole or trench. Pump removes the water as it accumulates and directs it into a piping system to a point removed from the home area. One or more sump pumps may be found in any one cellar area depending upon the extent of the problem. If the water-seepage problem exists and no sump pumps are employed, flooding with resultant damage to foundation, appliances, electrical system, etc., could result.

Survey—The process by which a parcel of land is measured and its area estimated. Also, the blueprint showing the measurements, boundaries and area of a property.

Swamp—An area of land generally wet, spongy and marshlike that may or may not be a good site for the construction of a pond or lake facility, depending upon various conditions necessary for these facilities.

Swimming Pond—A non-stagnant pond with proper depth (more than six feet at the center), not polluted and having a hard soil or rock bottom—not mud!

Tenant Farmer—A person who farms land owned by another and pays rent for the use of that land in cash, crops or services rendered to the landowner. Services might include maintaining lawns, gardens and buildings, mowing, plowing, fertilizing, etc. It is a very common practice today for owners of country property with large acreage of usable agricultural land to become involved in this type of arrangement with local working farmers.

Termites—Wood-boring worms or insects that are very

destructive to wooden structures. It is suggested that an expert be retained for the purpose of inspecting property to be purchased to determine if this problem exists. Location and control of termite problem should be matter of concern but not alarm. Effectively handled by professional firms if condition has not reached advanced stages.

Title—Evidence that the owner of land is in rightful possession thereof. Evidence of ownership.

Title Insurance—A policy of insurance that indemnifies the holder of any loss sustained by reason of defects in the title.

Title Search—An examination of public records to determine the ownership and encumbrances affecting real property.

Topography—The accurate and detailed description of land, with particular emphasis on surface features and elevations, including hills, valleys, rivers, lakes, roads, etc.

Under Contract—That condition or status of a pending real estate transaction representing the time beginning when purchaser and seller have respectively agreed to buy and sell under terms and conditions reduced to writing, but before actual transfer or closing. It is during this time that mortgage applications are made, surveys undertaken, title searches performed and legal documents prepared.

Underground Service—The type of installation that is installed from main source of public utility (electric, telephone, etc.) nearest the property to be served and is designated "underground service" because the wires, cables and piping are all placed in trenches below the earth's surface. This type of service is in contrast to overhead facilities where the wires and cables are strung directly from the source to a pole or corner of the building.

Village Property—Real estate available for purchase that is located within the confines of a small village or town and usually limited to one house, small barn or garage and less than one acre of land.

Volunteer Fire Company—A group of brave, dedicated, community-minded citizens who function in many rural areas without compensation, to protect the lives and property of the community from the hazards of fire and other catastrophes. Deserve wholehearted support by everyone residing in community in which they function. Extremely well trained and equipped.

Water Rights—The legal privilege granted to one not owning property on which the water facility exists, to use and/or take water for specified purposes that could include fire protection, human consumption, swimming, boating, fishing, and watering of animals. It should be a matter of concern to know whether such rights are in existence before purchasing property.

Water Softener—A most effective and widely used small tanklike apparatus usually installed in the cellar of a home for the purpose of removing the "hard" quality of water. As water enters the home from the well, it passes through the water softener containing certain chemicals and materials, before flowing to place of use. Minimum maintenance required. Costs vary with size but average approximately $350 installed for automatic type unit.

Water Table—The level below which the ground is saturated with water. This information is especially important to know before purchasing an existing property or building new structures. It is impossible in many areas to have a cellar because of water-table conditions. Supply of water from drilled wells is also influenced by water-table conditions in area.

Well—A flow of water from the earth obtained from a deep hole or shaft sunk into the earth for the purpose of finding an underground supply.

Wet Area—An area of land that is normally wet, muddy or soft especially during periods of rain, thawing or snow melting. A multitude of conditions could contribute to this condition, some of which are poor drainage away from area, underground springs, low and swampy ground, absence of topsoil, terminus of stream, brook or river. Inquiry should be made by purchaser of property to determine existence of such undesirable areas within the property limits.

Working Farm—Real property that is being used for agricultural purposes and may be assumed to have the necessary facilities, equipment and work force to function. It *does not* imply that it is operating efficiently or profitably.

Zoning Ordinance—An act of city or country or other authorities specifying type and use to which property may be put in specified areas.

27

THE COUNTRY VOICE

People in the country have not forgotten how to smile. Won't you join us?

Abandoned Railroad Track—Not used for anything but trains.

Abundant Water Supply—Near river.

All Stone House—I could have sneezed all night.

Amenities—Has electric lights.

Animals—Horse.

Architect—Whom you should have called in before—not after.

A Real Sleeper—Rip van Winkle.

Auction—Lots of people and expensive hot dogs.

Authentically restored—Requires a fortune to buy.

Back to Nature—Sleeping on the grass.

Being Sacrificed—Owner will cry all the way to the bank.

Boundary Line Agreement—Neighbors agree not to shoot one another.

Breathtaking View—Thirty thousand feet above sea level.

Carriage House—Why we bought the place.

Chalet—Slanting roof with balcony.

Character—Original builder was crazy.

Charm—Has tulip bed.

Close to the Road—No!

Colonial—Anything that isn't a ranch house.

Commuting Distance—The miles between Dr. Jekyll and Mr. Hyde.

Completely Renovated—Broken glass replaced with other broken glass.

Converted Studio—Installed skylight in roof. Cost only $79,500.

Country Kitchen—Four walls and an old sink.

Cultural Centers—Grange hall with bulletin board.

Currier and Ives Setting—Customer sees a painting of property without trailer court shown.

Dry Cellar—Lots of sponges on the floor.

Early American—The Lone Ranger's friend, Tonto.

Easily Accessible—Wells Fargo still serves area.

Excellent Value—Has grass.

Exclusive Area—Section occupied only by people and poodles.

Exposed Beams—No ceiling.

Extremely Liberal Financing—Bring lots of cash.

Fisherman's Paradise—Closet full of liquor.

Gentleman's Farm—No manure.

Golfing Privileges—Fifteen-dollar greens fee.

Good drainage—Big ditch.

Good Insulation—Old feed bags.

Good Shopping Facilities—The Avon Lady.

Guest Cottage—Old barn with indoor-outdoor carpeting.

Half-Clear, Half-Wooded—Present owner drinks Scotch in the morning and Bourbon in the afternoon.

Hand-Hewn Beams—Sculptures of yesterday carved with a hatchet.

Has Good Income—Next-door farmer rents land for one hundred dollars per year.

Heated Pool—Filter doesn't work.

Heavily Wooded—Truckload of lumber delivered to wrong house.

Hedge Against Inflation—Bush four feet high that needs trimming.

Historic—Wendell Willkie slept there.

Horse Farm—Phew!

Hunt Country—Gone to the dogs.

Hunting Preserve—Come up and shoot me sometime.

Ideal Retirement Home—Living room and dining room on first floor now bedrooms.

Inspection Report—386 things wrong with the property —fee $386.

Interesting Land—What *they* bought!

Interior Decorator—Every wife from the city.

Just Reduced—What happened to the seller's wife after joining Weight Watchers.

Leisure Home—No rest.

Log Cabin—What you said you wouldn't buy, but did.

Low Taxes—What the previous owner paid.

Many Extras—Light bulbs included.

Maven—The expert brother-in-law who manufactures ladies' underwear.

Minutes From Ski Area—Two hundred and forty minutes.

Modern Conveniences—Has doors.

More Land Available—Just nine miles away.

Mortgage application—Best-selling novel.

Mortgage Payments—Book-of-the-Month Club.

Mountain Retreat—Bring helicopter.

Near Waterfall—Twenty-six miles from Niagara.

Needs Work—Man! Does it ever!

Neighbors—Where?

New Listing—Property advertised for six months in *local paper*—that did not sell.

Old Mill—Barn without floors—no wheel.

Outbuildings—Two doghouses and a tent.

Owner Must Sell—Providing asking price is paid.

Owners Must Relocate—Couldn't afford the heating bill.

Pegged Floors—No nails.

Pine Forest—The new household deodorant.

Pollution—Local town board meeting.

Potential—H-m-m-m-m!

Pre-Revolutionary—Before the divorce papers were served.

Primeval Forest—Breeding area for rattlesnakes.

Privacy—Sunbathing in the nude.

Protected acreage—Swamp surrounds property.

Put Something of Ourselves Into—Blood, sweat, tears and *money*.

Quaint Home—No Closets.

Rare Gem—White elephant.

Realistically Priced—Are you kidding?

Recreational Areas—What the State Park had before it closed.

Remodeled Colonial—Has tiled floors, block ceilings—some paneled walls.

Retirement Community—Lots of prunes.

River View—Where is it?

Roads Through Property—Has driveway.

Rustic—John's last name.

Saltbox—Wear hard hats.

Seclusion—What your wife wants, until she has it.

Showplace—Wacky wallpaper and too many mirrors.

Small Mountain—Compost heap.

Small Orchard—Two apple trees and lots of bees.

Some Trees—two one-hundred-year-old elms, a hundred feet tall.

Some Water—Please?

Spacious Old Home—Several generations of mice.

Spring Water—$2.75 per gallon (delivered).

Stocked and Equipped—One cow and a garden tractor.

Structurally Sound—Termites have been removed.

Substantial Acreage—What the farmer next door has.

Three Fireplaces—Two without chimney, one behind the wall.

Tillable Land—Bring jackhammer.

Trout Stream—Loaded with snakes.

Unique—Just a plain mess.

Unspoiled—Has not been painted in sixty years.

Utopia—Mother will love it!

Vast Stands of Birches—Property adjacent to twelve members of the Birch family.

Vineyard—Three old boxes of grape containers.

Virgin Land—Trampled, but not touched.

Walking Distance—Please let me hear from you.

Water Frontage—Did *you* say three feet!

Wide-Board Floors—Cellar visible from main floor with accompanying creaking noise.

Wilderness Tract—What your mother-in-law thinks of your country place.

Windmill—Real estate salesman.

Woodchuck—Rabbit on hormones.

Year-Round Home—Has roof.

Year-Round Stream—No water for twelve full months.

28

END OF PREFACE

We are now coming to the end of our visit—which I sincerely hope will not end here, as I look forward to meeting many of you personally in the years to come.

It is the end of the book and you have concluded that our title, *Buying Country Property: Pitfalls and Pleasures,* was a misnomer, as we dealt mainly with the hazards.

Avoid the pitfalls and, believe me, the pleasure will be all yours!

Welcome to the Country!

INDEX

ABOUT THE AUTHOR

Irving Price was born and raised on a fruit and dairy farm in upstate New York. He received his primary education in a small country school, and went on to get a B.S. from Rider College in New Jersey, and to do postgraduate work at Cornell University.

During World War II he served with the United States Navy in the Pacific Theater for three years.

His twenty-five years of diversified real estate experience have not diminished the pleasure he finds in advising people about country property.

Broker, banker and builder, Mr. Price speaks with authority and wisdom.